'This book invites reflection on the nature of thought in relation to philosophical and analytic concepts of absence. Psychological practitioners have much to gain from this examination of thinking from the Greeks to the recent past.'

Lesley Murdin, *psychoanalytic psychotherapist in private practice in Cambridge and author of several books including* How Much is Enough? *and* How Money Talks

'This is a work of great reach and originality. The book will be invaluable to therapists wanting to deepen their understanding of psychic development. It will also be of real interest to those fascinated by the unconscious processes and roots of creativity — whether that is expressed through the arts or in a lived life. It explores the nature of containment that can lead to psychosis or to sublimation and inventiveness. The ideas put forward have implications for clinical practice and offer much food for imaginative thought.'

Maggie Murray, *psychoanalytic psychotherapist in private practice*

'A refreshingly new look at the foundations of psychoanalysis in relation to the philosopher Alfred North Whitehead, who turns out to be more than relevant. Deep thinking from a contemporary psychotherapist, practicing in a greatly changed world.'

Jenny Pearson, *psychoanalytic psychotherapist and dramatherapist and author of several books including* Analyst of the Imagination, the Life and Work of Charles Rycroft *and* Discovering the Self through Drama and Movement, the Sesame Approach

The Emergent Container in Psychoanalysis

Drawing largely from the psychoanalytic ground of Jung, Bion and Winnicott, from Plato and Whitehead and from numerous clinical studies, this book explores 'Absence' and 'Future' in the context of their many emotional and conceptual meanings.

Bringing together absence and future with Plato's concept of the 'receptacle' as described in the *Timaeus* and with Whitehead's handling of it, the author examines containment in psychoanalytic process. Here Jung's concept of 'container' (Tavistock Lectures, 1935) is in an ancient and continuing tradition of process thinking. The term 'emergent container' has been coined as the metaphorical and metaphysical space where the interplay between potentiality and actuality meet in the process of emergent reality. As absence emerges, experience consciousness develops, as well as the potential for symbolic thinking. In this sense, the experience of absence is considered as a potential container for and of creativity. If absence does not emerge as experience, there often follows the compulsion to fill emptiness with hallucination. Absence as it plays into the experience of containment is a key factor in the developmental and psychoanalytic process.

The Emergent Container in Psychoanalysis offers an exciting prospect for further research by psychotherapists and philosophers interested in the field of contemporary psychoanalytic thinking within and beyond their discipline. The book is also of great value to the inquisitive reader open to an exploration of human nature not confined to a single body of knowledge.

Ana Martínez Acobi is a practising Psychoanalytic Psychotherapist in North West London. She was born in Spain in 1967 and moved to London in 1986 where she studied and trained. Her interest lies in studying the unity of metaphysical and psychoanalytic thinking.

Philosophy and Psychoanalysis

Philosophy & Psychoanalysis is dedicated to current developments and cutting-edge research in the philosophical sciences, phenomenology, hermeneutics, existentialism, logic, semiotics, cultural studies, social criticism, and the humanities that engage and enrich psychoanalytic thought through philosophical rigor. With the philosophical turn in psychoanalysis comes a new era of theoretical research that revisits past paradigms while invigorating new approaches to theoretical, historical, contemporary, and applied psychoanalysis. No subject or discipline is immune from psychoanalytic reflection within a philosophical context including psychology, sociology, anthropology, politics, the arts, religion, science, culture, physics, and the nature of morality. Philosophical approaches to psychoanalysis may stimulate new areas of knowledge that have conceptual and applied value beyond the consulting room reflective of greater society at large. In the spirit of pluralism, Philosophy & Psychoanalysis is open to any theoretical school in philosophy and psychoanalysis that offers novel, scholarly, and important insights in the way we come to understand our world.

Titles in this series:

Psychoanalysis, Catastrophe & Social Action
by Robin McCoy Brooks

Metaphysical Dualism, Subjective Idealism, and Existential Loneliness: Matter and Mind
by Ben Lazare Mijuskovic

The Emergent Container in Psychoanalysis

Experiencing Absence and Future

Ana Martínez Acobi

Routledge
Taylor & Francis Group

LONDON AND NEW YORK

Cover image: Getty Images

First published 2023
by Routledge
4 Park Square, Milton Park, Abingdon, Oxon OX14 4RN

and by Routledge
605 Third Avenue, New York, NY 10158

Routledge is an imprint of the Taylor & Francis Group, an informa business

© 2023 Ana Martínez Acobi

British Library Cataloguing-in-Publication Data
A catalogue record for this book is available from the British Library

Library of Congress Cataloging-in-Publication Data
Names: Martínez Acobi, Ana, author.
Title: The emergent container in psychoanalysis : experiencing
absence and future / Ana Martínez Acobi.
Description: New York, NY : Routledge, 2022. |
Series: Philosophy & psychoanalysis | Includes bibliographical
references and index.
Identifiers: LCCN 2022017181 | ISBN 9781032200064 (hardback) |
ISBN 9781032200040 (paperback) | ISBN 9781003261841 (ebook)
Subjects: LCSH: Expectation (Psychology) | Psychoanalysis.
Classification: LCC BF323.E8 M428 2022 | DDC 150.19/5--dc23/eng/20220729
LC record available at https://lccn.loc.gov/2022017181

ISBN: 978-1-032-20006-4 (hbk)
ISBN: 978-1-032-20004-0 (pbk)
ISBN: 978-1-003-26184-1 (ebk)

DOI: 10.4324/9781003261841

Typeset in Times New Roman
by Taylor & Francis Books

Contents

Acknowledgements

I wish to give to Arthur Sherman, Jungian Analyst, my gratitude for the presence he has in the making of this book from beginning to end. His breadth of experience and dedication in the consulting room and his lifetime passion for the thinking of Plato, Whitehead and Jung, coupled with his inquisitive, innovative and critical thinking have made our conversations over the years and the writing of this book an exciting project. Calling him a collaborator would be short of his contribution to this book. Thank you Arthur.

I also wish to thank my patients for the fertile soil of experience and material they bring to the work, and for allowing me to use some of it in this book. Clinical material reproduced with permission of patients.

My gratitude also goes to Routledge for allowing me to use some extracts from: *Psychology of the Transference*, Jung, C. G. (1946), copyright (1983), Routledge imprint. Reproduced with permission of Taylor & Francis (Books) Limited UK through PLSClear.

Introduction

This book, *The Emergent Container in Psychoanalysis: Experiencing Absence and Future*, studies the ground between metaphysics and psychoanalysis. It is an exploration of 'absence' and 'future' as two dimensions of analysis. It is proposed that they meet in the concept of emergent container, and that this has potential for psychoanalytic research and practice. The author has coined the term 'emergent container' to denote its dual nature both as destructive and creative, as well as its holding function of diverse psychological states of mind and its potential for renewed creativity. She has long thought that there is a need for a concept such as 'emergent container' which recognizes the inner and outer realities together of these two dimensions. And she thinks that they can best be understood in unity in their influence on one another.

Absence is considered as a word between two worlds of experience and conceptual thinking. The former refers to lived experience with all its complexities, the latter to concepts such as negative capability, formlessness and empty space. It is proposed that if the experience of absence is contained, it is also propelled forwards. From the raw emotional experience of absence springs the emergence of consciousness. In that sense, the miracle of absence enables the miracle of consciousness (Arthur Sherman), as well as the potential for symbolic thinking and the discovery of the new. Absence is also considered as the very essence of the human condition, that is, as a fundamental property of psychic life and equally as the precursor to pathological organization.

Absence, hallucination, future, negative capability, container, emergence and experience are unifying themes. These areas are examined within the framework of contemporary psychoanalytic

DOI: 10.4324/9781003261841-1

thinkers: Freud, Klein, Winnicott, Bion, Green, Bollas and others, and largely through the lens of Plato, Whitehead and Jung, along with an extensive foundation of clinical material. The author has chosen two thinkers for this study because they bring philosophical process thinking which is paramount and parallel to Jung's thinking and contemporary psychoanalytic thinking, as well as providing interpretative frameworks for them. She believes this potential meets an ever-present need and opportunity for reflection and could well be called the 'Emergent Occasion' as did the poet John Donne (1694) in *Devotions upon Emergent Occasions* in its dilemmatic opening to experiential knowledge. This complementary approach carries potential for a deeper awareness of psychological and metaphysical dimensions. Both emergence of awareness and awareness of emergence in practice are the main concerns of the author's work.

In the opening chapter Plato's *Timaeus* takes centre stage, as well as providing the foundation for the whole book. In *Timaeus*, Plato (1965) equates absence with illness – the missing fourth – and views this absence in its dual nature both as destructive and creative. This absence, he describes as the 'receptacle': 'the nurse of all becoming and change'. This leads into an examination of Whitehead's handling of Plato's receptacle within his metaphysics and, thus, in process terms. Then the author likened Plato's and Whitehead's views of the receptacle to Jung's concept of 'container' (container–contained) as conceptualized in his treatment of the alchemical opus, from which he developed his ideas about individuation. She thinks that amongst Jung's most significant contributions are both the 'container' and 'future', and that future as myth and myth as future was behind his myth of Self and individuation. From Jung's concept of container the author moves towards Bion's theory of thinking which, as in *Timaeus*, emerges out of awareness of absence, and the interplay between container–contained and paranoid–schizoid and depressive position. For Bion it is the mechanism of projective identification that enables the origin of the capacity to think but also of pathological hallucination. Interwoven in the material and throughout the whole book she further explores the potential of normal hallucination for growth and the detrimental effect of pathological mentation.

In Chapter 5 the author explores absence from another dimension; from what Keats (1817) calls 'negative capability' which refers to "the capacity of being in uncertainties, mysteries and doubts, without irritable reaching after facts and reason". Against this background, negative capability is likened to reverie, to Jung's *abaissement*, to Bion's 'psychoanalytic faith', and to his suggestion to carry out the work 'without memory or desire'. It is further examined through Milner's 'pregnant emptiness', and Winnicott's notion of the therapist 'needing to fail his patients', in other words, through controlled catastrophe.

For Socrates and Plato the aim of life is to know yourself, yet Socrates's (*Cratylus*) (Plato, 1997) highest achievement was in reaching ignorance: "I only know that I know nothing". Socrates and Plato had grasped that the truth man knows is not of what 'is', but of what is happening. Bion, along similar lines, posited that 'O', the ultimate reality, cannot be known, but must be 'been'.

These ideas about existence and ultimate reality lead to Chapter 6 where following Whitehead's and Plato's ideas, experience is explored as process, and as ultimate reality whose basis is emotion. It is proposed that if the basis of experience is feeling, leading to cognition, then, the only way of organizing experience must be an immanent one: from within subjective feeling itself. Psychoanalysis can then be understood as a lure for feeling, an emotional experience, an adventure, where "blind emotion received and felt elsewhere in another occasion is conformally appropriated as a subjective passion" (Whitehead, 1929, p. 162). Viewed from this angle, the primitive level of experience is empathy. Empathy is a powerful way of knowing 'other' in psychoanalysis; it cannot be disputed, it is a given experience. If for Whitehead man's 'being' is constituted by its 'becoming', for Plato (*Timaeus*, 1965) the world of time "is a process of becoming and perishing and never really is". Both Whitehead and Plato follow Heraclitus's dictum: "No man can step in the saome river twice, for it is not the same river and he is not the same man". However, Whitehead adds to Heraclitus's dictum by describing not only fluency in being and experience, but also two kinds of fluency. One is concrescence – it becomes concrete, actualized – the other is from particular existence to particular existence: "the many become one, and are increased by one" (Whitehead, 1929, p. 21). This is Whitehead's way of thinking about absence.

Thinking about being and becoming leads the author towards absence. The missing fourth in *Timaeus* is further studied in relation to Jung's notion of the *quaternio*, to alchemy in *tetramenia* and in the 'Axiom of Maria', and to Whitehead's notion of what something 'is not' as the essence of what something 'is'. It is in this light that Winnicott's (1971) concept of the transitional object as the first 'not-me' possession, Bollas (1987) transformational object, and Andre Green's (1983) 'dead mother' concept is looked into.

Absence as both formlessness and empty space is considered in Chapter 10 in relation to emergent container which is the matrix of all things but is itself formless, to Jung's archetypes and to mutual unconsciousness. They are also likened to Winnicott's therapeutic procedure, which is to afford opportunity for formless experience, and for creative impulses which are the stuff of playing, and to Whitehead's (1929, p. 105) ideas for whom "Spontaneity arises from empty space, and life itself is a characteristic of empty space". Psychoanalysis rests on the premise that at the core of human nature lies a formless something, a Self, a mystery, and it seeks both to solve and to preserve this mystery.

The final chapter examines another aspect ubiquitous to human nature: the fact that interrelations are always present in man's existence. Psychotherapy is a lure for feeling. Feeling is relational. Relations are precognitive and affective. Each thing arises out of its social relations. This is what Whitehead calls 'causal efficacy', that is, the sense of derivation from immediate past, and of passage to an immediate future. The affective connections are intrinsic to the very core of any experience in space and time. Everything is interconnected to everything else, events are entirely interdependent, yet also mutually independent. The world and the world of emotions are both a disjunctive multiplicity of discreet entities, and a continuum web of interconnections. "Process and individuality require each other" (Whitehead, 1938, p. 97). The receptacle, as discussed in *Timaeus*, is the way in which Plato conceived the many experiences of the physical world as components of each other. It is Plato's doctrine of the medium of interconnection and intercommunication of all things. "The receptacle imposes a common relationship, but does not impose what that relationship shall be" (Whitehead, 1933, p. 150). It is what allows for process with retention and connectedness and enables all possibilities.

Psychoanalysis is the investigation of relationships through a relationship, and it attempts to open both partners to the emergent experience.

References

Bollas, C. (1987). *The Shadow of the Object: Psychoanalysis of the Unthought Known*. London: Free Association Books.

Donne, J. (1694). *Devotions upon Emergent Occasions. Meditations* XVII. Oxford: Oxford University Press, 1975.

Green, A. (1983). *The Dead Mother*. Edited by K. Mollon. London: Taylor & Francis e-Library, 2005.

Keats, J. (1817). *The Complete Poetical Works and Letters of John Keats*. Cambridge: Houghton Mifflin Harcourt, 1899.

Plato. (1965). *Timaeus and Critias*. Translated by D. Lee. London: Penguin.

Plato. (1997). Cratylus. *Plato Complete Works*. Edited by J. M. Cooper and D. S. Hutchison. Indianapolis: Hackett Publishing.

Whitehead, A. N. (1929). *Process and Reality*. Corrected ed. D. R. Griffin and D. W. Sherburne, Eds. New York: The Free Press, 1985.

Whitehead, A. N. (1933). *Adventure of Ideas*. New York: The Free Press, 1967.

Whitehead, A. N. (1938). *Modes of Thought*. New York: The Free Press, 1968.

Winnicott, D. W. (1971). *Playing and Reality*. London: Pelican Books.

Chapter 1

Absence and Future

Introduction

This first chapter explores 'absence' and 'future'. It is proposed that they meet in the concept of emergent container, and that this has the potential for psychoanalytic research and practice. The term 'emergent container' has been coined to denote its dual nature both as destructive and creative, as well as its holding function of diverse psychological states of mind and its potential for renewed creativity. The emergent container is evaluated throughout in its different aspects of relevance: as receptacle, as absence, as reverie, as formless form, as archetype, as symbol formation in process.

It is suggested that the concept of container is archetypal and ontological and a crucial one for psychoanalytic understanding and practice. The author proposes that absence is the very essence of the human condition; that is, that it is a property of psychic life and that depending on how the infant or adult deals with the emotions evoked in and by absence, it will influence a benign or pathological outcome. The emotion evoked in and by absence is the key, the compulsion to fill absence with hallucination, fantasy and/or imagination. But, of course, this will also depend on the capacity of containment to receive and modify the distress and terror associated with both absence and emergence.

The author has drawn from Plato and Whitehead because she believes, and attempts to demonstrate, that their 'process thinking' – process as experience and vice versa – is paramount and parallel to both Jung's and to contemporary psychoanalytic thinking, as well as providing interpretative frameworks.

DOI: 10.4324/9781003261841-2

Plato's Receptacle

Here Plato's *Timaeus* takes the centre stage as a prelude of what is to follow. In *Timaeus*, Plato equates absence with illness – the missing fourth – and views this absence in its dual nature both as destructive and creative. This absence, he ascribes to the 'receptacle': 'the nurse of all becoming and change'.

Plato's *Timaeus* is conventionally referred to as rhetorical display or presentation, not a philosophical dialogue, of the creation of the world and of human beings. It follows on from a previous conversation they'd had the day before, when Socrates and another four figures engaged in Socrates's presentation about the Ideal Constitution, the Ideal Rulers, and the Ideal City (this was Plato's famous *Republic*). Socrates had entertained Timaeus, Critias, Hermocrates and Glaucon and now it is up to them to entertain Socrates.

One, two, three, but where is the fourth, asks Socrates as he realizes that one of his guests of the previous day is missing. Thus begins *Timaeus* which is arguably one of the most powerful openings in Western literature. Timaeus replies that he has fallen ill for otherwise he would have never willingly missed today's discussion. Socrates entreats Timaeus and his companions to fill in for his absent friend. Timaeus consents, praises Socrates for his fine presentation of the previous day, and offers his own and their best performance in return (Plato, 1965).

Psychoanalysis traces the human experience of absence developmentally and archetypically; to the beginning of life, to birth and infancy and before, to the collective unconscious of man – the vast known and unknown of what was there before the person was born is a great part of what makes him possible. In several ways one's own sense of Self bears the imprint of its prenatal plenum. According to C. G. Jung (1875–1961), the Self is the archetype of wholeness and the regulating center of the psyche; a transpersonal power that transcends the ego. The Self signifies the unification of consciousness and unconsciousness in a person; that is, it designates the whole range of psychic phenomena in man. For Jung, the Self is an encompassing whole which acts as a container.

Early on in psychoanalytic thinking, Freud said that babies hallucinate the absent breast, in order to cope with the anxiety and internal fears which this absence brings about, a survival mechanism where

Freud emphasized the repression of absence and all the unbearable feelings it brings about; that is, the relegation of absence and its accompanying feelings to the unconscious. Similarly M. Klein (1882–1960) investigated the rich world of unconscious phantasy, where the infant's earliest mechanism to cope with absence and the persecutory anxiety that it creates are dealt with by splitting, for the absence is not just an absence, it is an absence filled with bad presences. The feelings evoked in and by the absence are the key. In psychological absence, as W. R. Bion (1897–1979) was well aware, psychotic anxieties and primitive defence mechanisms are activated in the infant, and re-activated in the adult.

Through Freud, Klein and Bion one learns that both the initial repression and splitting are a healthy start to cope with chaos, the emotional turmoil, and the terrifying fear of imminent annihilation, the 'nameless dread', that infants and patients alike experience, only to slowly and gradually – and aided by the containing function of the mother, or the therapist – be able to move on from the hallucinatory state, from the world of phantasy, or from the paranoid–schizoid position towards the depressive position, where the good and the bad can be brought together in relationship to the same internal and external object and the Self, and where the absence, sickness, distress and reality can be tolerated with a huge potential for the infant and for the patient.

This is not a straightforward movement and infants and adults alike can easily reverse back and forth between benign and more pathological states of existence. The individual has a huge resistance against the new. There is a tendency to employ psychological defences against pain, and one tends to hang on to something in order to avoid the unbearable feelings associated with absence. This is the main difficulty for the emergent container to emerge for it is not a happy story, it is a painful one. Emergence itself can be considered as the absence which partakes of beauty and terror. I have coined the term 'emergent container' to denote its dual nature as both destructive and creative, as well as its holding function of diverse psychological states of mind and its potential for renewed creativity. The emergent container is also the meeting point of 'absence' and 'future' as two interrelated experiences in analysis.

Most psychoanalytic and analytic thinkers have recognized through their own experience and work that it is out of pain, out of distress, out of suffering, out of sickness, out of chaos, out of absence that the human psyche is propelled to unconsciously fill with something that bears the imprint of psychopathology, or of mental well-being. It can go either way. When presented with a traumatic situation, the mind can either dissociate from such an appalling experience or struggle to make sense of it – both to make sense of it and of one's responses to it. The present discussion about absence represents a filling of the experience of absence with words and speculations. How else we might ask could we talk about psychological absence when absence is sheer emotion. In the feeling of absence, we can get stuck on hallucination and fantasizing and thereby get further and further away from reality, or we can move into a phantasy world of imagination and creativity. It is the latter that Jung emphasized.

All the main ingredients are already present at the opening of *Timaeus*, like a first session with a patient where most of the difficulties and potential to be worked through over the following years are explicitly and implicitly present. The principle ingredient is absence, which Plato equates with illness – the missing fourth – and equally crucial is the need to live with absence in the best way one possibly càn. Similarly, in psychoanalytic work, the analytic couple is constantly working in, working with and working through, absence, the void, the caesura, emptiness: that human experience which is so present within and between patient and therapist, and which often manifests as emotional distress, as a constant and devastating experience of abandonment. The patient has to suffer this precarious and terrifying state of internal affairs and, depending on how he or she can cope, will influence a benign outcome or a pathological one. The emotion evoked in and by psychological absence is the key, the compulsion to fill or cure absence with hallucination, phantasy and/or imagination.

Paradoxically, it is this absence and this sickness that carries with it all potential for development; the psychological and emotional upheaval is inseparable from mental growth. The potential of void pulls the person into the beginnings of civilization, but it also carries with it all potential for sickness and pathology. It is this absence which is both most destructive and most creative, which Plato describes in *Timaeus* as the receptacle: 'the nurse of all becoming and change' (TimaeusPlato, 1965, p. 67, para. 49). It is contemporary with the discovery of the new. It is the receptacle, or the potential for symbolic thinking by which I mean emergence. It is what enables the miracle of absence; for there is no consciousness without the emergence of recognition of absence. There is no thought without the awareness of absence. Absence must be felt and in being felt it distresses because it introduces rupture in our being. This creates anxiety which, if it becomes unbearable, the mind will try to obliterate and get rid of by evacuative methods. If, on the other hand, anxiety is noted and tolerated, it has an opportunity to become thinking material, leading to awareness of reality and beyond. In that sense, the miracle of absence enables the miracle of consciousness, and that this process should take place at all is itself a miracle, given the psychological pain and suffering that it involves. Plato says that nothing actually left it and nothing entered from anywhere – there was indeed nothing else – and it nurtured itself procuring its own destruction, whereas all that it suffered and did in itself and by itself happened by art. He who created it felt indeed that it would have been better if it would have been self-sufficient and not in need of anything else.

In Jung's view, absence is the starting point of imagination and play; for the imagination of man and for the pursuit of man's longing for the transcendent, for wholeness. This process is enabled through relationship, through the mystic marriage or *coniunctio* between both the conscious and the unconscious mind, and patient and therapist. Patients project onto and into the therapist their shadow aspects, their unconscious contents, their sufferings and fears of absence and abandonment, and it is through the unconscious infection that therapeutic possibility springs.

Quoting from Jung (1946, p. 165):

> The transference phenomenon is without doubt one of the most important syndromes in the process of individuation: its wealth of meaning goes beyond likes and dislikes. By virtue of its collective contents and symbols it transcends the individual personality and extends into the social sphere, reminding us of those higher human relationships which are so painfully absent in our present social order, or rather disorder. The symbols of the circle and the quaternity, the hallmarks of the individuation process point back, on

the one hand, to the original and private order of human society, and forward on the other to an inner order of the psyche.

This is a psychological process which involves fluidity from transference to transcendence.

But, it is also the absence that can become the receptacle for the rigidity of concrete thinking: the 'Claustrum' of which Meltzer (1992) speaks. That is, a pathological world of hallucination, claustrophobia and delusion which are, in essence, a denial of absence. Through analytic and psychoanalytic work, the therapist constantly finds himself immersed in this absence and sickness that Plato so clearly intuited and understood. For example, the therapist has breaks, he offers 50 minutes session; he is not always emotionally available in the ways that patients need him to be. He misrepresents, misunderstands, gets absent-minded, preoccupied, and sometimes he cannot reach patients at times of utter desolation and isolation. In short, the therapist himself becomes the absence.

In Winnicott's (1963) terms 'we constantly fail our patients', and it is precisely through this absence and through this failure that therapists help, that they are good enough.

The womb, the breast, the mother, therapists, are not quite ready at all times and, as in *Timaeus*, what was readily available yesterday, today is missing; and all patients can do, and patient and therapist in a relationship can do, is to live with it, to live through it and to survive. The absence is always present. Yet, simultaneously, it is not just about surviving. It is about therapists being the receptacle, the container for living; for living one's life to its full potential. In the *Symposium*, Diotima says to Socrates that all men are bringing to birth in their bodies and their souls. There is a poetry, which as he knows, is complex and manifold. All creation or passage of non-being into being is poetry or making, and the processes of all arts are creative: and the masters of all arts are poets or makers. What are they doing who show this eagerness and heat which is called love? The object which they have in view is birth in beauty. For Whitehead (1929, p. 348) "God and the world are the contrasted opposites in terms of which creativity achieves its supreme task of transforming disjoined multiplicity with its diversities in opposition to concrescent unity, with its diversities in contrast". In other words, it is a transformation into beauty.

Timaeus itself is a myth-making of creation. It is a working through things out of nothingness – that is, out of absence; all that it suffered and did in itself and by itself happened by art. Its first lines start with absence in the form of sickness and then it goes on to describing the creation of the world – from absence to the creation of the universe and the world of humanity, which is for Plato one and the same thing: absence as the nurse of all becoming. Plato's notion of receptacle is akin to Jung's 'container' (container–contained).

Whitehead's View of Plato's Receptacle

The exploration of Plato's receptacle leads to an examination of how this concept comes into Whitehead's own as he conceptualizes it within his metaphysics. For Whitehead, the receptacle, is a dynamic vessel of interrelations and personal unity; the metaphorical space where the process of reality takes place. Identity for Whitehead involves the relationship between being and becoming going on in the receptacle. Whitehead (1933, p. 187) states:

> In addition to the notions of the welter of events and of the forms which they illustrate, we require a third, personal unity. It is a perplexed and obscure concept. We must conceive it the receptacle, the foster-mother as I might say, of the becoming of our occasions of experience.

Whitehead borrows Plato's metaphor of the receptacle as the 'foster-mother' of the becoming of our existence. Plato himself uses the term interchangeably with 'the nurse of all becoming and change', both terms conceiving the receptacle as involved in the process of novelty and creation. Both Plato and Whitehead conceive the receptacle in process terms.

For Whitehead, being and becoming are part of the process of existing, therefore no ontological dichotomy exists between them. However, he, as Plato, needs to account for the passage from being to becoming. This transition involves a dynamic interplay between the many and the one, absence and presence, chaos and order, indetermination and determination, potentiality and actuality. For Whitehead, the receptacle is the metaphorical vessel where connections and transformations occur; it is the metaphorical space where past, present and future, and the potential and the actual meet in the ongoing process of reality and identity formation. This personal identity is for White-head what receives all occasions of the person's existence and functions as a natural matrix for all transitions of life. For Whitehead, personal identity is an awareness of unity within the general unity of nature. It is a process of unification and of explaining how sameness arises in socie-ties which remain themselves while undergoing change, thus constituting personal identities. In the process of unification past realizations are transferred into the present where they acquire a new individual form, shaped by the ingression of a selected eternal object. An 'eternal object' for Whitehead is a potentiality for actual entities and is selected in the light of the actualization of future potentialities. Eternal objects invest the datum with the individuality of the subject. Whitehead presupposes a datum which is met with feelings, and gradually attains the unity of a subject: objectivity is absorbed into subjectivity.

For Whitehead, the receptacle is the matrix of pure relationship, the metaphysical space where the process of reality takes place and where the connection between what is actual and what is non-actual – past and potential – meet. Whitehead (1933, p. 181) puts it thus: "The present moment is constituted by the influx of the *other* into that self-identity which is the continued life of the immediate past within the immediacy of the present". The receptacle enables the meeting between present and 'other' which includes all that enters into the constitution of an actual entity without itself being actual. This dialogue paves the way for novelty since prehensions give rise to new occasions. In this sense, the receptacle is for Whitehead the vessel for pure relatedness and novelty.

At times, Plato seems to privilege being over becoming. The Platonic ideal Forms are for him the non-physical essences of all things which are timeless and unchanging. On other occasions, Plato speaks of the Forms as poles of relations or qualities that keep transforming. In this sense, they are relational processes in which different characteristics emerge. Similarly, Plato's phenomenal bodies are not complete, enclosed substances but transforming relations. These views are akin to Whitehead's process view of reality. However, as a consequence of Plato's inconsistent views and evolving thinking, it may sometimes appear that for him the receptacle is mainly the physical locus of intermediation, while for Whitehead it is the very matrix of connections and the space where decisions are made.

For Plato, neither the Forms nor the receptacle nor the phenomenal bodies are constituted by any substratum or inner form. The receptacle is invisible, formless and all receptive, yet his notion of the receptacle seems to indicate a kind of underlying synthesis. Whitehead's receptacle preserves something of Plato's receptacle's character regarding underlying synthesis when he speaks of 'mutual immanence' from which individualities can emerge. Whitehead (1933, p. 150) states: "The Receptacle imposes a common relationship on all that happens, but does not impose what that relationship shall be". The receptacle is the dialectic setting for occasions, the space between and within occasions, not the occasions themselves. In this sense, Whitehead's receptacle is closely connected to Winnicott's (1971) concept of the 'transitional space' where things are in-transit and where the object is both 'me' and 'not me' simultaneously. It refers to becoming and to what one experiences as process into experience.

For both Plato and Whitehead, the receptacle is the general unity of Nature. For Whitehead, our own sense of identity pervading our life-thread of occasions is nothing other than awareness of a particular aspect of unity within the general unity of Nature. Similarly, for Plato, the receptacle is the whole. In *Timaeus* (1997, pp. 1254–1255, para. 52b) Plato says that the Receptacle is

> that which keeps its own form unchangingly, which has not been brought into being and is not destroyed, which neither receives into itself anything else from anywhere else, nor itself enters into anything else anywhere. It is invisible – it cannot be perceived by the senses at all – and it is the role of understanding to study it.

For Plato, nothing enters and nothing leaves the receptacle and, thus, it can only nurture itself procuring its own destruction, whereas all that it suffered and did in itself and by itself happened by art. He, the craftsman, who created it felt that it would have been better if it would have been self-sufficient and not in need of anything else. For Plato, the receptacle and Nature itself embodies the whole and thus it encompasses destruction as well as creation. Whitehead (1933, p. 150) says:

We speak in the singular of *The Universe*, of Nature, of physis, which can be translated as Process. There is one all-embracing fact which is the advancing history of the one Universe. This community of the world, which is the matrix of all begetting, and whose essence is process with retention and connectedness – this community is what Plato terms the Receptacle.

For Whitehead, Plato's intuition of the Receptacle as the 'foster-mother of all becoming' or 'the nurse of all becoming and change' suggests that Plato conceived it as a necessary notion for any analysis of Nature. Similarly, for Whitehead, the receptacle contains all actual and potential occasions, as well as the past, present and future and thus, it encompasses both ontology and teleology. As the metaphysical aspect in the process of identification, the receptacle is closely linked with the overall process that contains all the single processes and their possibilities.

Even though neither for Plato nor for Whitehead is there an ontological dichotomy between being and becoming, both were confronted with the problem of reconciling these two dimensions of existing. The receptacle meets this need for it is in this metaphorical vessel of relations that decisions are made and values selected. In Whitehead's (1933, p.187) words: "That which happens in it is conditioned by the compulsion of its own past, and by the persuasion of its immanent ideals". In other words, an event is both conservative and creative; a particular history of events repeated in the present at a specific moment in time and space and, simultaneously it is already propelling forwards towards future events – towards something new and different from what it was. The receptacle is the metaphysical space where relatedness, unification and identity take place and where each new creation announces future ones.

Jung's Concept of Container Is Akin to Plato's Receptacle

Plato's and Whitehead's views on the receptacle lead to likening them to Jung's concept of 'container' (container-contained) as conceptualized in his treatment of the alchemical opus, from which he developed his ideas about individuation. What this means is that for Jung a psychological vessel is what enables conscious and unconscious minds to meet, transform and transcend. Jung's container as Plato's receptacle is a metaphorical vessel which encompasses absence and future. Jung's psychology and Plato's and Whitehead's philosophy are concerned with the teleology that they hold to be inherent experience. The model of the container–contained runs silently through Jung's work as a central motif in his treatment of the alchemical opus, but it finds its full expression in three seminal papers. Jung's development of his concept of container is examined through these three seminal papers: 'Marriage as a Psychological Relationship' (1925); 'The Tavistock Lectures' (1935) and 'The Psychology of the Transference' (1946).

Marriage as a Psychological Container

The concept of the container as such appears for the first time in Jung, described as 'the problem of the container and contained' in his paper 'Marriage as a psychological relationship', published in German in June 1925 and translated into English in 1931. Here Jung states that the greater the area of unconsciousness, the less is the marriage a matter of free choice, in the sense that the marriage choice will normally follow the unconscious motivations of instincts. Unconsciousness results in non-differentiation or unconscious identity. The consequence of this is that one person presupposes in the other a psychological structure similar to his own. This state can be described as one of complete harmony and a return to an original condition of unconscious oneness of childhood. But, for Jung, this is more than a mere return, or repetition of an already experienced state of affairs, it also points to the future and to the new. It is a return to the mother's womb, into the teeming depths of an as yet unconscious creativity which transcends, obliterates and consumes everything individual. It is a real communion with life and manifests the impersonal power of fate.

For Jung, one can only speak of an individual relationship in the psychological sense when the nature of the unconscious motivations – the biological instinctual goal: the preservation of the species and its collective nature – has been recognized and the original identity broken down.

It is important to remember that Jung is talking about both marriage in the common use of the term, that is, marriage between two people, and about the marriage of the conscious and unconscious mind within the Self. Progressive mental development means, in effect, extension of consciousness. It is with the rise of a continuous consciousness, and not before, that a psychological relationship with oneself and with another becomes possible, but this psychological birth is not always pursued or achieved, for the journey is treacherous. It involves pain, absence, chaos, void and loss – what Socrates (*Theaetetus*) called 'the labours of birth', including the recognition that large areas of psychic life will always remain unconscious.

In this passage, Jung explores in detail the symbolic meaning of the vessel and the connection of the container symbol with the magic circle, a ritual image that Jung further extends to the mandala, which he describes as a means of protecting the centre of the personality, the Self, from being drawn out and influenced from both outside and inside.

The idea of the vessel – which, as a receptacle, suggests the action of containing, in order to hold together something that would otherwise fall apart – is an archetypal one.

The vessel – the receptacle, the container symbol, the mandala, the magic circle – is also represented in matrimony by the exchanged rings: the circle of trust.

For Jung, the ways that lead to conscious realization are many, but they follow definite laws. In general, the change begins with the onset of the second half of life. The middle period of life is a time of enormous psychological importance. The real motivations are sought and real discoveries are made. The critical survey of oneself and one's fate enables the person to recognize his/her peculiarities. But these insights do not come to him easily; there is no birth of consciousness without pain.

There is a tendency in the human mind to avoid change and therefore to linger in the youthful attitude, but the aims of the second half of life are different, and this situation produces a division of the will and a massive conflict ensues. This disunity with oneself begets discontent, and since one is not conscious of the real state of things, one generally projects the reasons for it onto one's partner. A critical atmosphere develops – the necessary prelude to conscious realization.

According to Jung, it is almost a regular occurrence for a woman to be wholly contained, spiritually, in her husband, and for a husband to be wholly contained, emotionally, in his wife. It is important to note both that the situation could as easily be reversed, and that one partner is not completely the container and the other the contained, that is, both are container and contained for, and of different aspects of, the other. This is what Jung describes as the problem of the 'contained and the container'. The one who is contained feels himself to be living entirely within the confines of his marriage, the container, on the other hand, cannot be absorbed into the contained, but encompasses it without being contained.

The more the contained clings, the more the container feels shut out of the relationship. With the onset of middle-age, what might have started as an unconscious awakening, develops into a more conscious state of affairs when one realizes that one is seeking completion, seeking the contentedness and undividedness that has always been lacking. The absence becomes noted and real, and if one has not done so already, one might be looking elsewhere to fill that void.

For the contained this is only a confirmation of the insecurity he or she has always felt so painfully; the hope of security vanishes, the fourth is missing, and what there was available yesterday, no longer is. As is often the case, the conflict can go either way. In other words, at this juncture one's disappointment may drive one to desperate and violent efforts in forcing one's partner to capitulate, or to admit to his childish phantasy of a longing for unity, or it may drive one in on oneself. If the latter, one's acceptance of failure may do one real good, by forcing one to recognize that the security one was so desperately seeking in the other is to be found in oneself. In this way one finds oneself and discovers in one's own simpler nature all those complexities which that container had sought for in vain.

Mrs. C, a middle-aged woman with two grown-up children, presented for therapy after her husband had been urging her to do so for a couple of years. Her husband's complaint was that she has a controlling nature both towards him and towards the children and thus, he demanded of her to work through her problem in therapy. From the beginning of the therapy, the marital problems were re-enacted in the transferential relationship between us. For example, the sessions were completely swamped by her incessant talk and, invariably, right at the end of the session, she would ask my direct advice on how to deal with the particular difficulty discussed. I felt the pressure: the feeling of being shut out of the relationship. With time – a lot of time and patience – the dynamics of what was happening between us, as a parallel to what was taking place in her marriage, were discussed and grasped in situ. As a consequence, a lot of personal history and early abandonment came to the fore, including her need since an early age to find a container for such varied and fragmented feelings. Mrs. C is a highly intelligent and practical woman, but she is cut off from her own feelings. My sense is that her early experience of abandonment by her own mother, and a busy father, led her to unconsciously repress her painful feelings, for there was no significant figure emotionally available to contain them.

A year into the therapy, her husband announced that he wanted to separate, and a few months later, that there was another woman waiting for him: a sweetheart from high school, with whom he had been corresponding for some time. Mrs. C felt betrayed and devastated. Her bitter complaint included the fact that she 'took her husband in' twenty-five years ago, when he was socially awkward, and that she had 'transformed him' into a more socially acceptable character. She has always felt proud of herself for this, but now she feels resentful that, in the process, a reversal seems to have taken place and it is she herself now who is insular and socially uninvolved. She also resents that she sacrificed her profitable career, in order to give herself fully to her marriage and to the upbringing of their children. Not to mention the fact that she started therapy reluctantly, and, initially, only in order to comply with her husband's exigency. As she put it 'she came to therapy in order to solve their marital problems'. She is in shock, hurt and humiliated.

Her initial reaction in learning about his wish to separate, and then, the existence of another woman, was to try to win him over. But, meanwhile, in the therapy, she is also working on herself, and becoming more aware of her own nature within and beyond her marriage; her shortcomings as well as her strengths. By now, as painful as her discoveries are, she knows that their differences are insurmountable, that they have probably always been, and that her future entails fears and perils, but also that this is an opportunity to become her own person. She is going through a difficult time, since the world as she knew it has been shuttered (what there was yesterday is no longer available, as in Plato's *Timaeus*), but she is also beginning to realize that a dissociation is not healed by being split off, but by more complete disintegration. Amid her emotional turmoil, she resists and fears further disintegration, but she is also becoming conscious of the possibility of an inner integration, which before she had always sought outside herself. This is the meaning of the emergent container in its dual aspects: the container as absence, loss and painful process, and as potential growth and future.

Another patient, Mr. J, has been working through these conundrums in his therapy with me for some time. His negativity towards his wife (contained) was becoming more openly expressed in our sessions, as opposed to being acted out at home with his wife – drinking excessively and having anger outbursts. At the same time, he was gaining insight into the fuller disintegration that his psychological growth required. His wife too was perceiving, if not understanding, the internal turmoil her husband was going through, and somehow, intuitively, this felt to her even more distressing than their previous disagreements. Unexpectedly (and not), Mr. J arrived for a session and announced that his wife had given him an 'ultimatum'; it was either therapy or her. Mr. J recognizes the claustrophobic nature of his marriage, he is not happy, and even envisages the rupture of his marriage in the near future but, instead, and with felt emotion, he decided to give up his therapy.

The transformation, or potential transformation, that Jung describes, is the very essence of the psychological marriage relationship: marriage as a psychological container, as an emergent container, if allowed to be worked through all the way to its ultimate consequences, including the projection of certain archetypal images, primarily anima and animus. These primordial images have an extraordinary positive value, but they are also responsible for blinding fantasies and the likelihood of the most absurd aberrations. Mrs. C continues to work through this conflict and is gaining renewed realization of the psychological relationship that marriage brings. In this case, the projection though dangerous itself is helping her pass from a collective to an individual relationship, and from a tremendous suffering to an emergent future. Her journey of discovery continues to be tumultuous and challenging, frustrating and liberating, and she seems to be developing a profound empathic response towards herself. Having said that, one should be cautious in isolating consciousness from either or both subjective psyche and collective psyche. This is the danger of which Whitehead (1929, p.7) speaks of as 'misplaced concreteness', for the psyche is a unit that is interacting all the time. The psyche is a receptacle, a container, holding diverse information, personal, impersonal, conscious and unconscious experience. It is a process, as Plato, Jung and Whitehead so clearly understood. Mr. J., on the other hand, resisted going through the conflict and retreated to the familiar status quo.

The Container as Vessel, as Receptacle for All Aspects of Self

Jung continued to develop his concept of the container – a concept akin to Plato's receptacle – and his labours shone through in 1935 when between 30 September and 4 October he delivered the so-called 'Tavistock Lectures'. These lectures were recorded in shorthand and appeared in England in 1968. In the fifth and last of his lectures, Jung's remarks on the psychological meaning of a container hold a particularly prominent position. Jung used two pictures painted by a schizophrenic patient to illustrate his point to the audience. Both figures (1968, Figure 14 and 15) show a vase. Jung explains how the schizophrenic patient was trying either to find or to make a receptacle to collect all his (disparate) psychic elements. These pictures, according to Jung, are the psychotic's attempts at self-cure, with the aim of bringing together again all the disparate elements resulting from the splitting processes of the schizophrenic illness.

After Jung had explained the meaning of the German word 'Gefards' and arrived at the function of 'containing', he characterized the symbol of the vessel as the receptacle for his whole being, including the incompatible parts. This is a task which the ego would have been unable to perform since it can only identify and deal with one part at a time, whilst what he needed was a container for everything. The notion of the receptacle, the container, is vast and a little vague, and yet, as Jung calls it, it is the 'vase mirabile' – the miraculous retort, the ultimate container. This is what I call 'the emergent container', and is one of the most valuable concepts the therapist has – a vessel for psychological states of mind which would otherwise be scattered, fragmented or dissociated. Without a psychological container, mental fragmentation would take place in every one of us, including the less disturbed and the more chronic patients, as well, for whom curing becomes nursing, and nursing the receptacle: the nurse of all becoming and change (Plato, 1997).

In the fifth lecture Jung explores in detail the symbolic meaning of the vessel and the container symbol with the magic circle and the mandala which he describes as a means of protecting the centre of the personality – the Self. This receptacle, container, vessel, temenos, sacred precinct, or mandala serves to protect from both spilling and intrusion of psychological contents. As Jung had previously done in 'Marriage as a Psychological Relationship' (1925), he emphasizes that the idea of a vessel which, as a receptacle, suggests the actions of containing in order to hold together something that would otherwise fall apart, is an archetypal one. The temenos is understood as a psychologically charged area surrounding a complex; a container which may be expressed as either a womb or a prison, that is, in its positive or negative aspects. Indeed, one finds under the banner of container such varied, akin and antagonistic terms as receptacle, vessel, vase, mandala, temenos, sacred place, bath, sanctuary, process, analysis, claustrum, cloister, oyster, enclosure, disclosure, closure, foreclosure, opening, den, liar, dungeon, prison, coffin, etc.

Jung observed that in Goethe's *Faust* (1808), Goethe is really describing the experience of the alchemist who discovers that what he has projected into the retort is his own darkness.

The psychological process is essentially the same: the becoming aware of these powerful contents which alchemy sensed in the secrets of matter. The mandala definition from Goethe's *Faust* goes as follows: "Formation, transformation, the eternal mind's eternal recreation". And that is the Self, the wholeness of the personality, which, when everything is well, is harmonious, but which can bear no self-deception. Similarly, Jung's mandala images were cryptograms on the state of his Self, which were delivered to him each day.

In Goethe's *Faust*, Mephistopheles is addressing Faust, giving him directions to the realm of the Mothers, that is, to the realms of the depths of man, to his unconscious. Mephistopheles states:

A glowing tripod will finally
show you
that you are in the deepest,
most deepest ground.
By its light you will see the
Mothers:

the one sits, others stand and
walk,
as it may chance. Formation, transformation,
the eternal mind's eternal
recreation.
Covered in images of all
creatures,
they do not see you, since they
only see shades.
Then hold your heart, since the
danger is great,
and go straight to that tripod
touch it with the key!

The image of woman too, represented as the 'anima' by Jung, of whom the first personification is the mother, is also a sort of vase, for in the beginning she incorporates the whole of the unconscious, instead of being scattered in all its various units (Jung, 1935). Here Jung hints at the function of the mother at the beginning of life and her significance to the body – her all-important function of, as a container, gathering together and holding the unconscious contents evacuated by the subject.

It is important at this juncture to emphasize that Plato's receptacle, Whitehead's receptacle, Jung's container and my notion of emergent container, are more than a developmental concept related to the infant–mother relationship. In other words, that these concepts go beyond and cannot be reduced, to psychoanalytic 'Object-Relations Theory', for they incorporate the functions of containing, enabling and transforming not only developmentally, but also archetypically and metaphysically.

One may find it interesting, if anecdotal, that while Jung was exploring the significance of the container concept in his work, his wife, Emma Jung, quite independently from him, was immersing herself in the teachings of the holy grail – the holy cup for some, and the holy mother for others.

Container as Alchemical Process

Jung (1946), based on the Alchemical process, pays special attention to the painful and transforming process necessary for the emergent container to emerge; for the transformation via psychic infection or empathy that the two people involved in the therapeutic relationship need to go through. The painful process begins with the *nigredo* or *tenebrositas* which is described by the alchemist as the *separatio of diviso elementorum*, the *solutio, calcinatio, incinerato*, or *dismemberment* of the body; while this extreme form of *disiunctio* is going on, there is a transformation of the *arcanum* – be it substance or spirit – it invariably turns out to be the *mysterious Mercurious*. In other words, out of the monstruous animal forms, there gradually emerges a *Rex simplest*, whose nature is one and the same and yet consists of a duality (Goethe's 'united dual nature'). The alchemist tries to get round this paradox or antimony with his various procedures and formulae, and to make one out of two – this is the same process as in the individual psyche. But the very multiplicity of his symbols and symbolic process proves that success is doubtful. Seldom does one find symbols of the goal whose dual nature is not immediately apparent. His *filius philosophorum*, his *lapis,* his *rebis,* his *humunculus* are all hermaphrodite. His goal is not *vulgi*, his lapis is spirit and body and so is his tincture, which is *sanguis spiritualis* – a spiritual blood. One can understand why the *nuptiae hymicae*, the royal marriage, occupies such an important place in alchemy as a symbol of the supreme and ultimate union, since it represents the magic-by-analogy which is supposed to bring the work to its final consummation and bind the opposites, by love, for love is stronger than death.

For Jung, alchemy describes, not merely in general outline, but often in the most astonishing detail, the same psychological phenomena which can be observed in the analysis of unconscious processes. The individual's specious unity that emphatically says, 'I want', 'I think' breaks down under the impact of the unconscious. So long as the patient can think that somebody else (his father or mother) is responsible for his difficulties, he can save some semblance of unity (*putatur unus esse!*). But once he realizes that he himself has a shadow, that his enemy is in his own heart, then the conflict begins and one becomes two; there is an 'obfuscation of the light'. In other words, consciousness is depontiated and the patient is at a loss to know where his personality begins or ends. It is like the passing through the valley of the shadow, says Jung, and sometimes the patient has to cling to the doctor as the last remaining shred of reality. This situation is difficult and distressing for both parties; often the doctor is in much the same position as the alchemist who no longer knew whether he was melting the *mysterious amalgam* in the crucible or whether he was the salamander glowing in the fire.

Psychological induction inevitably causes the two parties to get involved in the transformation of the third and to be themselves transformed in the process, and all the time the doctor's knowledge, like a flickering lamp, is the one dim light in the darkness.

For Jung, this is in the highest degree true of psychoanalytic work. A genuine participation, going right beyond professional routine, is absolutely imperative, unless of course the doctor prefers to jeopardize the whole proceeding by evading his own problems, which are becoming more and more insistent. The therapist needs to go to the limits of his possibilities, otherwise the patient will be unable to follow suit. Arbitrary limits are not of use, only real ones. It must be a genuine process of purification where 'all superficialities are consumed in the fire' and the basic facts emerge. The alchemical process, alike the psychoanalytic process must indeed be a difficult and painful process of mutual transformation through relationship, kinship libido and empathy. Therapists must fully participate in this process and allow themselves to go through hell together. This is the real meaning of the container which they provide, and of the emergent container which they create.

Jung (1946) asks:

> Is there anything more fundamental than the realization, this is what I am? It reveals a unity which nevertheless is-or-was a diversity. No longer the earlier ego with its make-believes and artificial contrivances, but another 'objective ego', which for this reason is called the 'Self'. No longer a suitable fiction, but a string of hard facts, which together make up the cross we all have to carry or the fate we ourselves are.
>
> (p. 35)

Regarding the cross we all have to carry, Jung reminds us that nobody who finds himself on the road to wholeness can escape that characteristic suspension which is the meaning of the crucifixion. For he will infallibly run into things that thwart and 'cross' him: first, the thing he has no wish to be (the shadow); second, the thing he is not (the 'other', the individual reality of the 'you'); and third, his psyche non-ego (the collective unconscious). This process underlies the whole opus, but to begin with is so confusing that the alchemist tries to depict the conflict, death and rebirth figuratively, on a higher plane, first – in his *practica* – in the form of alchemical transformations and then – in his *theoria* – in the form of conceptual images. In psychotherapy and in the psychology of neurosis it is recognized as the psychic process par excellence, because it typifies the content of the transference neurosis. The supreme aim of the *opus philosophorum* is conscious realization.

For Jung, the alchemists more than anybody else were the first to feel the true needs of man, for, as psychotherapists, they had the most direct dealings with the sufferings of the soul. Whilst endorsing Jung's view, one may also add that much before the alchemists, Socrates and Plato (in the Western world) were grappling with the true needs of man and the sufferings of the soul: the pains of labour as Socrates called it.

Regarding the fate that we ourselves are, Whitehead's views are relevant. According to Whitehead (1938, p. 117),

> Some facts have such closeness of reference to the immediate self that our intimate unity with them is claimed. In this way, the concept of self-identical enduring personal existence dawns. It is the concept of one person with many stages of existence.

When some facts have such closeness of reference to the immediate self that an intimate unity with them is claimed might be another example of what Whitehead (1929, p. 7) calls "the fallacy of misplaced concreteness". Thus, to use another of Whitehead's phrases: "The many have not become one, nor have they been increased by one", but instead, the many is mistakenly taken to be one. We are both one person with many stages of existence and, simultaneously, a fragmented self in unity. The real meaning of the *coniunctio* with oneself and with another ('other') is that it brings to birth something that is one and united.

Jung understands the pictures of the alchemists regarding the *coniunctio* as the union of the biological level of the symbol of the *unio oppositorum* at the highest. This means that the union of opposites in the royal art is just as real as coitus in the common acceptance of the word, so that the opus becomes an analogy of the marital process by means of which instinctual energy is transformed, at least in part, into symbolic activity. Psychoanalytic work, like the alchemical opus, is the container for transformation. This is the type of higher transformation that Diotima brings about in Plato's *Symposium* through her conversation with Socrates, and it is also represented in Goethe's 'higher copulation', both of which could be compared with the primitive, initial state of chaos, the *massa confusa*, or rather with the state of *participation mystique*, where heterogenous factors merge in an unconscious relationship.

> No more shall you stay a prisoner
> wrapped in darkest obfuscation;
> new desires call you upwards
> to the higher copulation.

In 1917, Jung wrote a chapter on 'The Sexual Theory' in the *Psychology of the Unconscious Processes*, which presented a critique of the psychoanalytic understanding of the erotic. In his 1928 revision of this chapter, retitled 'The Eros Theory', he added that the erotic belongs on the one hand to the original drive nature of man. On the other hand it is related to the highest form of the spirit. It only thrives when spirit and drive are in right harmony. "Eros is a mighty daemon", as the wise Diotima said to Socrates, "He is not all of nature with us, though he is at least one of its essential aspects". In the *Symposium*, Diotima teaches Socrates about the nature of Eros. She tells him:

> He is a great spirit, Socrates. Everything classed as a spirit falls between god and human.
> What function do they have?, asked Socrates.

> To which Diotima replied: They interpret and carry messages from humans to gods and from gods to humans. They convey prayers and sacrifices from humans, and commands and gifts in return for sacrifices from gods. Being intermediate between the other two, they fill the gap between them and enable the Universe to form an interconnected whole. They serve as the medium for all divination, for priestly expertise in sacrifice, ritual and spells, and for all

prophecy and sorcery. Gods do not make direct contact with
humans, they communicate and converse with humans (whether
awake or asleep) entirely through the medium of spirits.

(Plato, 1951, p. 81)

Jung (1961) reflected on the nature of Eros, describing it as 'a
kosmogonos', a creator and father–mother of all consciousness. This
cosmogonic characterization of Eros needs to be distinguished from
Jung's use of the term to characterize woman's consciousness.

Jung emphasizes (thereby also criticizing Freud's approach to psychoanalysis) that if one approaches this task with psychological views
that are too personalistic, one fails to do justice to the fact that one is
dealing with an archetype, which is anything but personal. It is a priori,
a universal. That is, animus/anima represent the 'trans-subjective' union
of the archetypal figure. Therefore, the 'Jungian' transference cannot be
just understood at the level of personal history, but archetypically. The
archetype always stands for some typical event and these archetypal
images give meaning to the irrational foundations of the patient's
transference. For Jung, the carrier of the projection is not just any
object, but it is always one that proves adequate to the nature of the
content projected – that is to say, it must offer the content a 'hook' to
hang on. This explains why the projection usually has some influence on
the carrier, which is why the alchemists in their turn expected the 'projection' of the stone to bring about a transmutation of base metals.

In analytic work too, the psychoanalytic relationship, receptacle or
container enables the transmutations of base metals into gold, that is,
the transformation of primitive, instinctual and biological feelings and
drives into symbolic representations. However, one might question the
assumption of the 'hook' on the receiver. Of course, there needs to be a
hook, otherwise the projection could not be received and worked
through and, of course, it goes without saying that without a hook
transformation in both participants will not be possible. However,
projections are the ways of the psyche, they are constantly taking place
across the board till it finds a container, a receiver, an empathic recipient, in the same way that Bion (1977) postulated the existence of
'thoughts without a thinker', that is, thoughts in search of a thinker.
This notion refers to the fact that at times the person is not quite ready

to think about something, while at other times he is more receptive to it. But it is doubtful that calling it a 'hook' is always helpful, in the sense that if the projection is pathological, one is also implying the pathology of the therapist, which may or may not be the case. There is a danger in misunderstanding, or another example of misplaced concreteness in Whitehead's terms. After all, therapists and patients share being human, they share archetypes, and the therapist, through the exercise of intuition in his work is emotionally and empathically attuned and connected to his patients. In other words, the 'hook' is the very essence of empathy and, on occasions, one may run the risk of pathologizing one's innermost asset: the container itself.

According to Jung, the first indicators of a future synthesis of personality, appear in dreams or in 'active imagination', where they take the form of the mandala symbols which were also known in alchemy. But the first signs of this symbolism are far from indicating that unity has been attained. Just as alchemy has a great many very different procedures, ranging from the sevenfold to the thousandfold distillation, or from the 'work of the day' to 'the errant quest' lasting for decades, so the tensions between the psychic pairs of opposites ease off only gradually; and, like the alchemical end product, which always betrays its essential duality, the united personality will never quite lose the painful sense of innate discord. Complete redemption from the suffering of this world is and must remain an illusion. The goal is important only as an idea; the essential thing is the opus which leads to the goal: that is the goal of a lifetime (in its attainment, conscious and unconscious work in harmony). The work is the emergent container, and so is the Self.

Regarding the latter, Jung reminds us that the artist does not act from his own creative whim, but is driven to act by the stone. This almighty taskmaker is none other than the Self. The Self wants to be made manifest in the work, and for this reason the opus is a process of individuation, a becoming of the Self. The Self is the total, timeless man and as such corresponds to the original spherical bisexual being who stands for the mutual integration of conscious and unconscious. The Persian Gayomant is as broad as he is long, hence spherical in shape, like the world–soul in Plato's *Timaeus* – like a mandala. Thus, the Self can be viewed as a containing concept, as the receptacle, the container and organizer of all opposites, and the transference as the emergent container for individuation.

References

Bion, W. R. (1977). *Taming Wild Thoughts.* London: Karnac.

Goethe, J. W. (1808). *Faust.* London: Penguin Classics, 2005.

Jung, C. G. (1917). The sexual theory: Psychology of the unconscious processes. *Collected Works*, vol. 7.

Jung, C. G. (1925). Marriage as a psychological relationship. *Collected Works*, vol. 17.

Jung, C. G. (1928). Revision of the Eros theory: Psychology of the unconscious. *Collected Works*, vol. 7.

Jung, C. G. (1935). The Tavistock Lectures. *Collected Works*, vol. 18.

Jung, C. G. (1946). *The Psychology of the Transference.* Translated by R. F. C. Hull. London: Routledge, 1983.

Jung, C. G. (1961). *Aniela Jaffe: Memories, Dreams and Reflections.* New York: Random House, 1963.

Jung, C. G. (1968). Analytical psychology: Its theory and practice. *The Tavistock Lectures. Collected Worksh*, 18. London: Routledge & Keegan Paul, 1977.

Meltzer, D. (1992). *The Claustrum.* London: Karnac.

Plato. (1951). *The Symposium.* Translated by W. Hamilton. London: Penguin.

Plato. (1965). *Timaeus and Critias.* Translated by D. Lee. London: Penguin.

Plato. (1997). Timaeus. *Plato Complete Works.* Edited by J. M. Cooper and D. S. Hutchison. Indianapolis: Hackett Publishing.

Whitehead, A. N. (1929). *Process and Reality.* Corrected ed. by D. R. Griffin and D. W. Sherburne (Eds.). New York: The Free Press, 1985.

Whitehead, A. N. (1933). *Adventure of Ideas.* New York: The Free Press, 1967.

Whitehead, A. N. (1938). *Modes of Thought.* New York: The Free Press, 1968.

Winnicott, D. W. (1963). Dependence in infant-care, in childcare, and in the psychoanalytic setting. *The Maturational Process and the Facilitating Environment.* London: Karnac, 1990.

Winnicott, D. W. (1971). *Playing and Reality.* London: Pelican Books.

Chapter 2

Hallucination as Pathology and as Entrée into the Collective Unconscious

Introduction

Thinking about receptacle and container leads to potential outcomes. When we cannot bear absence or tolerate much reality, there is a pull to reverse back to hallucinatory states of mind. Hallucination can be either or both an opening into the unconscious (personal and collective), into novelty, into consciousness and into thinking, but also into a claustrophobic and persecutory state of existence. In other words, hallucination can become concretized thought and feeling that gets lost, or else, it can be imagination. Jung emphasized hallucination as imagination as he realized that hallucination provided an opening into the collective unconscious and the most pressing of all concerns: the evolution of the Self archetype. For Jung, hallucination reflected the irreducible inner reality and the aim to compensate a one-sided ego attitude towards life. Hallucination is more than a kind of reparative phase of psychosis meant to restore the world of objects lost or destroyed in phantasy. The person's experience of absence leaves a void wherein one participates in symbolic actions of representation and rebirth. Absence and its concomitant hallucination is (or can be) separation and individuality growing out of identity. Empathy is considered as the capacity to enter the hallucinating mind to understand 'at-onement'.

Absence as Potential for Growth and for Pathology

Although as human beings we are innately predisposed to tolerate some degree of absence, we cannot bear absence. Absence feels too real, and too much reality becomes intolerable, and thus, very quickly

DOI: 10.4324/9781003261841-3

we start to fill in. In the place of absence one often puts church, text, theory, etc. It does not matter what the individual is given, he reverses back to hallucinatory states. He is constantly destroying what he has got, for the emergence, as the absence brings with it both beauty but also terror. Images are understood in the context they are found in. The feelings, the emotion evoked in and by absence continually draw us on and are always the key. Absence impacting as experience is emergence (Arthur Sherman).

Jung (1927) provides some clinical material about a man who was suffering from a paranoid form of schizophrenia. He became ill in his early thirties. He had always presented a strange mixture of intelligence, wrong-headedness and fantastic ideas. He was an ordinary clerk and as a compensation for his very modest existence he was seized with megalomania and believed himself to be a saviour. He suffered from frequent hallucinations and was at times very disturbed. He said that he had to look at the sun with eyes half-shut so that he could see the sun phallus. What he did not know and, according to Jung, he could not have known, is that this image was part of the Mithraic Cult.

What this example and many such like it made Jung realize is that hallucination provided an *entrée* to dialogue with the collective unconscious and the most pressing of all psychic concerns: the evolution of the Self archetype. For Jung, hallucination reflected the irreducible inner reality with its own claims and reasons. In a broad sense, such irruptions aim to compensate and expand (or destroy) an overtly constricted personal and ego-attitude towards life.

In a similar vein to Jung, Marion Milner (1957) writes of a 'pregnant emptiness', a no-mind state of being that allows the new to enter. Milner's 'pregnant emptiness' is also closely connected to Winnicott's chaos and unintegration. But then, the fear is one of breakdown. Similarly, for Jung, the archetype of creativity requires tolerance of absence and of emergent internal objects – Jung's encounter with the unconscious.

But, does one allow for play and playfulness, and for integration to emerge, for a sense of a true Self to emerge, or for the emergent container to emerge, or does one need to abort the venture of self-discovery by prematurely organizing defences and filling-in the empty space? One may also question which is more basic – 'absence' or 'chaos'. For Whitehead, our world was not created out of absolute nothingness, but emerged out of primordial chaos. And yet, the chaotic state is the nature of empty space, since it is the thusness of absence that creates the primordial chaos.

It would appear that it is the absence, the missing fourth, that one has difficulty with, as opposed to the mere reduction of pain as Freud intimated, since hallucinations tend to maximize experience in both heavenly and hellish directions and so, cannot be clearly tied up to pain reduction.

Furthermore, one often observes that it is equally or even more traumatic and damaging having had experienced emptiness, void, absence of emotional human contact than actually having been exposed to abuse (of course, the nature and the extent of the abuse is of the essence, and one would not wish to underestimate the impact on the psyche). What is important to emphasize is that due to some forms of psychological, emotional, physical, or sexual abuse, the person/patient often still loves and hates the perpetrator, particularly if he or she is a family member, that is to say, there is an emotional bond or connection, even if an ambivalent one, while when the infant, child or adult has been emotionally abandoned, psychological growth ceases to take place altogether. In Winnicott's terms (1971), the infant has reached the X, Y and Z of its limits and has now completely disconnected from a world of emotion and human contact.

Green's (1983) book, *The Dead Mother*, describes a situation when the mother is physically present, but emotionally absent – depressed or emotionally unavailable. The trauma consists of a prolonged absence of affective interaction and how the child responds to this traumatic disruption, or to this absence that always was; the infant often responds by a malignant identification with the emotionally dead mother. His identification with a dead mother who is incapable of loving contributes to a corresponding incapacity to love others and to love oneself. There is also a relative incapacity to regulate affect. This is based on the recognition that in infancy homeostatic processes are mutually regulated (Beebe et al., 1977; Shore, 1994). This disturbance in affect regulation may arise from a non-specific asynchrony in the mother–child relationship, consistent with Jung's and Bion's theory that the mother is the container and initial possessor of the child's anxiety.

Some have argued that the findings of infant research cannot be directly transported into adult psychoanalysis and offered as a causal explanation for adult psychopathology. This position also includes a tendency to deprecate Freud's belief in historical reconstruction. However, the persistent influence of the affective memories of the mother–child interaction, implicit in the dead mother syndrome/complex, is a direct challenge to this view. In other words, the absent mother has permeated the whole of the human being personality and continues to manifest in adulthood through lack of friendships, lack of motivation, absence of relationships, of zest for life, etc. The 'unthought known' (Bollas, 1987) of maternal emotional absence makes its presence in every aspect of personality and experience.

Absence and Its Concomitant Hallucination as Separation and Individuality Growing out of Identity

I mentioned earlier that for Jung, hallucination provided an entrée to dialogue with the collective unconscious and the most pressing of all concerns, the evolution of the Self archetype. But, what is hallucination? For some psychoanalysts, hallucination is no more than a perception of a memory of an actual satisfaction but, one could argue, in agreement with Jung, that hallucination contributes something new: it brings a new dimension into the equation, for it brings its own nature into play, and the inner reality of the individual. Hallucination is more than a kind of reparative phase of psychosis meant to restore the world of objects lost or destroyed earlier (in phantasy). The patient's experiences of absence leaves a void wherein one participates in symbolic actions of representation, repair, rebirth, etc. Absence is here seen as the growth of consciousness, which also reminds one of the void of future the patient enters one way or another. Absence and its concomitant hallucination is (or can be) separation and individuality growing out of identity.

Jung's primary question is the growth of consciousness and, of course, Eros – that is, the moment the mother–child dyad is formed and Eros is constellated. The present absence is included in Jung's *abaissement*, and, also, in Bion's 'memory, desire and understanding'. As pathology, absence takes form as blanking, confusion and schizoid remoteness; in exploration, as feeling the way in the dark. Consciousness is here understood as islands in the sea of the unconscious and the experience of absent object as the first thought, as found in Plato's *Timaeus* (1965).

What is generally called 'hallucination' in psychoanalysis could be called 'imaging': between images and imagination. Jung talks about images – including thought, language, action, visual images, words, ideas – all are images. Whitehead puts it more concisely: fallacy of misplaced concreteness affecting the thought processes. That is, articulation of feeling that gets lost in hallucination with credence without reason.

Whitehead, like Jung and Plato, considers absence as the emergent container, and the emergence of novelty as the all important crucial factor. Whitehead (1929, p. 161), states that "the general case of conscious perception is negative perception". In other words, "consciousness is the feeling negation" (what something is not). "Such feeling is in full development. Thus, the negative perception is the triumph of consciousness".

For Whitehead, the last delicacies of feeling require some element of novelty to receive their massive inheritance of bygone systems. Order is not sufficient. What is required is something much more complex. It is order into novelty so that the massiveness of order does not degenerate into mere repetition, and so that the novelty is always reflected upon a background of system. The old dominance should be transformed into the firm foundations, upon which new feelings arise, drawing their delicacies of contrast between system and freshness.

In conversation with Lucien Price (1956), Whitehead emphasizes the value of freshness and surprise in experience. Taking the example of good music, he says something to the effect that its beauty resides in that the unexpected interval surprises the ear and this effect endures even when the music becomes familiar. For Whitehead, we long for freshness in our lives and some of our most vivid experiences seem to have this perennial quality. This reverberates in other areas of experience so that when we are revitalized in one area it revitalizes us in others and, equally, when we feel rotten or dead in one area it crosses over to others.

The primacy of novelty, like very little else, did not escape Plato when in the prologue to *Timaeus* he stated: "from this source we have delivered philosophy, that which no greater good ever was, or ever will be given by the gods to mortal man".

The Absent Isle of Atlantis (*Timaeus*) as Conceptualization of Self

Here the myth of the isle of Atlantis is brought forth as symbolic representation of the struggles of the Self. *Timaeus* starts in absence – the missing fourth – then the story develops towards a second absence – the whole island disappears – before moving towards the creation of the world.

Before Timaeus embarks on telling his story as to how the universe and human beings came to be, Critias, a member of the four, relates an ancient story about the isle of Atlantis. And how she first rose to the leadership of the Greek cause and how, later on, forced to stand alone, deserted by her allies, she reached a point of extreme peril. Nevertheless, she overcame the invaders and erected her victory. She prevented the enslavement of those not yet enslaved and generously freed the rest of us. Some time later, excessive violent earthquakes and floods occurred, and after the onset of an unbearable day and night, the entire warrior force sank below the earth all at once, and the isle of Atlantis likewise sank beneath the sea and disappeared. This is how the ocean of that region has come to be even now unnavigable as the sea bed is covered by a layer of mud at a shallow depth, the residue of the island as it settled.

This awe-inspiring myth of Atlantis, once again, puts us in touch with our own nature as human beings: a feisty, resilient warrior within, a Self, a Soul ready to overcome internal and external adversity. But also a Self which when abandoned and deserted by its allies; when having to endure such extreme and unbearable forces by itself, sinks and disappears in actual death, or in a living death. And yet, it is not fully gone; a residue of non-navigable mud has settled.

This could be conceived as a metaphorical conceptualization of the unconscious. It is the absence of the whole island, or to put it another way, it is in the island that, once again, all future possibilities and potentialities reside. It is the residue that makes possible the miracle of the new beginning. The most destructive is the most creative.

Whitehead (1956) openly speaks of the explosive impact that absence, that is, what was there yesterday no longer being available, had in his whole being and in his entire works, mainly the philosophical texts. He demonstrates the infinite novelty which he has reached in his writings because of it.

Whitehead, as remembered by Lucien Price (1956), expresses the impact that the displacement of the Newtonian physics had on his whole being. The impact resides in the fact that the Newtonian physics were taught to him as a bed-rock of certitude and truth. Although Whitehead continued to value Newtonian ideas, he acknowledged that they were no longer true. It is this sense of being thrown from a place of certitude into inconceivable infinities that affected everything in the universe for him.

Further Thoughts on Hallucination

It was questioned earlier whether hallucination is a perception of a memory of an actual satisfaction, or whether it constitutes something of its own and, it would appear, in agreement with Whitehead, Jung and Plato, that it is not just the evoking of a memory, but that it brings something new to it.

Another relevant question may be whether one believes the original satisfaction was an 'actual' one, or an ideal phantasy. However, it seems that whether the hallucination is based on an original/actual experience, or an archetypal phantasy remains an open question, unanswerable unless understood as a couple mutually influencing each other.

As mentioned earlier, hallucination can be either or both an opening into the unconscious (personal and collective), into novelty, into consciousness and into thinking, but also into a claustrophobic and persecutory state of existence.

Jung (1935) makes a distinction between hallucination as claustrum, and phantasy as imagination. For example, imagination is the real and literal power to create images. It is the active evocation of (inner) images, an authentic feat of thought or ideation, which does not spin aimless and groundless fantasies 'into the blue' – does not, that is to say, just play with its objects, but tries to grasp the inner facts and portray them in images true to their nature. This activity is an opus, a work (true work) which demands that the individual conscientiously, accurately and carefully records and elaborates the content now pushing its way into consciousness. If, on the other hand, the intolerance of absence (note that human beings are all predisposed to a degree of tolerance of absence) is too great, the patient will fill in the analytic space with whatever is to be discerned from evolving emergence. This is the difference between defensive concrete and symbolic work. Intolerance of absence is the root of transference. Jung presumes this in much of his work on consciousness. Tolerance of absence brings about consciousness, and intolerance of absence promotes stagnation. If the latter is the case, the filling in will almost be inevitable, and a complex will appear. In that sense, a complex is here understood as the mind's attempt to compensate emptiness which characterizes readiness to experience.

Once again, the difficulty is staying with absence and emptiness, as opposed to filling it up, either with pain or with joy. In *Memories, Dreams and Reflections* (1961), Jung provides an account, a vision of an experience of waiting, of 'staying with' as holding container of emerging contents. The need to wait and 'stay with', as well as the unavoidable need for suffering, since it is out of need, pain and suffering that the new emerges, is also emphasized by Jung in the *Spiritual Problem of Modern Man* (1928). He says that it is from the need of distress that new forms of existence arise and not from idealistic requirement of mere wishes.

Necessity is the mother of all science, says the old adage.

Nietzsche's observation regarding suffering is that it may deepen a man, but does not make him better. It is important to add to this view, that there might be a danger of glorifying suffering – another fallacy of misplaced concreteness in Whitehead's terms. As with anything else in the human mind, suffering can go either way. In other words, suffering may deepen a man or may shut the man out. If the person is deepened by suffering, he may become a better person, for he is more aware of his darker aspects, of his own humanity and that of others, as opposed to those darker aspects having a free rein on him. But, by the same token, the deeper man is a more powerful man, for he knows his mind and that of others' better, and that can be used, manipulated and abused for sheer destruction, personal and otherwise.

Another qualification which it is important to make is that in talking about suffering, one is contrasting it with feeling pain. Many patients (or anyone, for that matter) are in pain, but not all of them suffer it, in the sense of feeling the pain of an absence – or the absence of fulfilment and desires in Bion's terms – enduring it, and making something out of it. The latter is what constitutes suffering as containment.

Suffering and Laughter as Containment

The psychoanalytic endeavour is a difficult one in which suffering is unavoidable since the individual has to face his own shadow, otherness, and separation from the collective unconscious. While acknowledging that there is something terrifying in the very birth of the self, the therapist also believes that one should not underestimate the importance of laughter for well-being. Bringing together suffering and laughter (non-hysterical laughter, that is) is another way of bringing the opposites together and thereby enabling the third: the Transcendent Function, in Jung's terms.

Whitehead deals with the 'necessity of irreverence'. In dialogue with, and as recorded by, Lucien Price (1956), Whitehead questions whether experience, cause, belief or anything else should monopolize the whole of life to the exclusion of laughter. For him, laughter is an instinctive burst, a compensatory regulator to a one-sided conscious attitude, an outburst of the irrational and a reminder that our theories are necessarily only an attempt to make our existence intelligible.

During a session a female patient was upset, crying. Her distress was related to a confusing situation regarding a newly established relationship with a man. She relates a recent episode of unspoken upset and frustration in both parties as a result of coitus interruptus at their first attempt at intercourse. We explored her feelings, what happened, what was happening between the two of us in the here and now, etc. We came to gain some insight about her frustration and anger (and possibly his), as well as our lack of (emotional) intercourse today in our session. As we worked through these feelings, something was emerging and the atmosphere began to feel slightly less tense, clearer and lighter. I felt that passive aggression might have played an important part in their unsatisfactory outcome. I pondered if all their rage, anger and frustration during the day had been directed to the actual sex act, and through sadistic – and sadomasochistic – withdrawal, rendering it impossible. I was about to ask: "Where do you think the aggression went?" But, instead, I uttered: "Where do you think the erection went?" My patient was roaring with laughter and, unavoidably, so was I. I tried to contain my own laughter and sustain the 'psychoanalytic attitude', but I could not keep a straight face. As she continued to laugh with all her heart, I felt ashamed, but healthily human and, above all, deeply connected with my patient. It really felt like a won-derful orgasmic emotional intercourse – symbolically speaking – between the two of us. When she recovered from her outburst, now mixed up with joyful tears, she said: "Write a paper". Once again, out of me it came: "Therapist cock-up". As one can imagine, the intensity of laughter in my patient at this point was beyond description.

For the rest of the session, we were able to reflect on the value of spontaneity; the need to be, and not let feelings bottle up, and the need to allow oneself to be chaotic and ridiculous in every relationship, including ours, as opposed to trying to keep it perfect and unreal. To start with I was mortified by my own sluggishness, but soon it became apparent that my own letting go of something and allowing for the unpredictable to emerge, seemed to have enabled my patient to do likewise, and for the two of us to share an intimate moment.

Empathy in Plato's Receptacle and in Jung's and Bion's Container

Here empathy is studied as the capacity to enter the hallucinating mind to understand 'at-onement'. Empathy is further studied in Chapter 6 in Whitehead's terms, that is, from the angle of internal relatedness.

Like Plato's receptacle, a contribution of Jung is container: from claustrum to receptacle. Following Jung, one must be prepared to move from one mental place to others. Jungian threshold is from unconscious to conscious, claustrum opening to receptacle, eternal presence (constant object) opening to miracle of absence (object constancy).

So quickly the container is filled by concrete description; so quickly it expands in symbolization and its multitude of possibilities. In con-tainer Jung has given us an intuitive concept as large or small as we need. From the concrete realism of denial of psychic reality to the mysteries of love and the *coniunctio*. Container is an intuitive concept that reaches into depths of analytic understanding, into the uncon-scious unknown.

The claustrum is closest to Jung's ideas of identity. As I will explore later, the desire to be understood is Bion's take on Melanie Klein's projective identification, and it is basic to Jung's container themes: in infancy, it is explored in forms of identification where the separation of opposites is avoided. The container as unconscious is 'the magic circle of nature', the temenos a psychologically charged area around a complex within which the opposites transform. Container expands as opposites differentiate. Symbolic meaning develops with container, that is, from unconscious identification to dreaming together.

For Jung, empathy is introjection, containing the patient, and a comparing with the analyst's experience. This is similar to reverie, that is, as mother/therapist capable of containing projective identification (which definition I will discuss later, in relationship to Klein and Bion).

Jung's take is *abaissement* and transcendent function as process in loosening identification with mother (container). What initially may have been a parasitic relationship results in change of perspective or attitude and then, chaos ensues – necessary for developmental growth. Jung's empathy relates to listening as interpreting, and interpreting as 'taking in', a subjective state of impact, reading the patient, as best information of the patient's state of mind. From this perspective, thinking and listening are co-terminus, in the same way that practice and theory are. This begs the question: 'What is clinical material?' If interpreting begins in the act of listening, 'clinical' and 'theoretical' begin together. Therapists should be aware of their own schisms.

The miracle of absence is a priori to waiting and hence to transcendent function, to concrescent experience (the 'selected fact' of Poincaré, 1952). Before absence (of good object), there is presence of bad (persecutory) object, and before that, the miracle of hallucinated object. In *Timaeus*, one sees the movement from absence to sickness to miracle of absence and, in alchemy, the transformation of the base metals into gold, or philosopher's stone, that is, differentiation of psyche and matter. From hallucination to meaningful vision; from hallucination which aims at immediate gratification to something greater which aims at satisfaction. Perhaps it could be argued that the most familiar form of hallucination is transference and countertransference.

According to Jung, and also to Bion, one needs to be capable of entering the hallucinating mind to understand, 'at-onement'. This is one way of describing empathy. This, as elaborated by Bion's and Klein's ideas, is an account of thinking. To start with, thoughts appear fused with body states and/or emotion. Thinking begins in absence, since thinking arises in spontaneous recognition of (thought of) absence (of absence of satisfaction) and works on painful thought.

Thinking begins in invisibles with representations of things that are absent. This is the miracle of absence – the miracle that works through absence and gives birth to the awareness of absence and thus, to the capacity for thinking and conscious awareness.

Concepts and theories are also assessed empathically. But, as can be seen in Bion's description, even more accentuated, thinking is also prevented from developing when attacks on linking predominate, that is, attacks on the thought that links, so that the hallucinatory state prevails. The internalization of mother/therapist as a thinking object is resisted if thinking is alien to the infant/patient in interpretations which are too theory based. Process as containment, and the reverse, is a notion opened by Jung.

Jung's Views on Future

Here I propose the view that Jung's views on future are closely connected to Whitehead's notion of the discovery of future and the potentiality of future.

I mentioned earlier that an important contribution of Jung to contemporary work is that of container, in the same way that Plato's akin notion was receptacle. However, it will be more accurate to say that Jung's most significant contributions are both the 'container', or what I have termed 'the emergent container', and that of 'future'. Future as a dimension of analysis is sometimes neglected in psychoanalytic discourse. Jung did not neglect it. Future is the 'what for?' question. While the 'why?' question addressed at any event, with a because answer can amount to a defence. The latter, however, is the familiar shape of many analysis and it ends where it begins; with its assumptions and concreteness. 'Always', 'never', are hallucinatory mood thoughts with which one fills the void of emptiness and then, omnipotence develops as a substitute for waiting for the appropriate realization to mate with the pre-conception (Bion, 1963).

Future is the 'what for?' question which opens emergent and symbolic dimensions, and denotes an evolving process. In this sense Jung's view on future cannot be limited to the 'what for?' question or any other question, but it is close to Whitehead's discovery of future and potentiality of future. The individual is in constant struggle between dead concrete and live symbol, container as prison or womb. The vas as analysis is the place of transformation. The psychoanalytic receptacle invites the presence of the unpredictable element within the psychological temenos; the sacred precinct within which a god's presence can be felt. The symbol is the receptacle (space) happening. The Platonic dialogue, or the psychotherapeutic conversation via speech is, in its duality, the filling of the receptacle and/or the making of it. Emotion as libido is the initial archetype. And analysis is a symbolic experience of unconscious material and hence, it activates archetypal transference which is then projected onto/into the therapist – from transference to transcendent. Transference itself is a word with two meanings; Freud's emotionally important person from childhood (personal unconscious) and Jung's aspect of Self (collective).

If, for Freud, past was the crucial factor, for Jung, future is. The person uses the void as a container when he projects future into it. In that respect, future can be symbolic or symptomatic of the unconscious, for one projects into it hopes, despairs, desires, phantasies, the present, the past. Desire fills the void with hallucinated future and thus, Bion's induction to approach the session with 'no memory or desire'.

For Jung, future as myth and myth as future was behind his myth of Self and individuation. Analysis as emergent container both creates and contains its evolution. If memory is the name of one's relationship with the past, so is intention with future, and interacts with present. For Jung (1927), the inherited future is all the future things that are taking place in him. Emergence, as well as erupting in terror, defences and somatic symptoms, awakens new visions beyond immediate fact, but this is intolerable to some. Absence, as the emergent container and the emergence of novelty, are the all important crucial factors. One's anticipatory state includes a desire for something, even if the something is not clearly defined or known. In the apparent calm of the consulting room, we face the evolution and emergence of the most primitive parts of the mind, the Self: the total, timeless man which embodies past, present and future. And, as in *Timaeus*, Jung's future as void, as void at the heart of things is his major insight which is not pessimistic, but, on the contrary, which is full of possibility. Plato's absence represents a void wherein the symbolic emerges, moved by Eros.

In the Kabbala god steps back from himself to create a void to see himself in: recognition of absence ... in which patient is symbolically present. Mandalas are birth places, as future, as void. The individual engages in the future, he does the future. Refusal to do so is pathology of growth, defences of Self, psychotic defences. The power of immanence (of the mind) is terrifying, if not participated in as intention, purpose, engagement – in short, as experience. The person distracts in phantasy, hallucination, blanking, all of which are psychotic defences of filling the void. One turns void into something persecutory or non-existent, meaningless and hence that cannot disappoint. Certainly some patients can fill a room (void) with emptiness. If tolerated it can become positive hallucination – dream of present. The future of future is infinity, and infinity is a big word to contemplate, let alone to endure. In void one has reached the highest level of abstraction, the zero that no event could qualify.

Analysis as emergent container both creates and contains its evolution. It is an important psychoanalytic task to enable a multifaceted and open-ended container, that is, to create an atmosphere that allows the patient to feel that in psychic life almost everything is possible, while simultaneously offering a sense of limit which deepens, sharpens, and makes the exploration safe. Void, receptacle, actuality, future cannot be internalized but, as unconscious is assimilated, unconscious grows – the demands of learning cannot be other than a continuous learning.

References

Bion, W. R. (1963). Elements of psycho-analysis. *Seven Servants*. New York: Jason Aronson, 1977.

Bollas, C. (1987). *The Shadow of the Object*. London: Free Association Books.

Green, A. (1983). *The Dead Mother*. Edited by K. Mollon. London: Taylor & Francis e-Library, 2005.

Jung, C. G. (1927). The structure of the psyche. *Collected Works*, vol. 8.

Jung, C. G. (1928). Revision of the Eros theory. Psychology of the unconscious. *Collected Works*, vol. 7.

Jung, C. G. (1935). The Tavistock Lectures. *Collected Works*, vol. 18.

Jung, C. G. (1961). *Aniela Jaffe. Memories, Dreams and Reflections*. New York: Random House, 1963.

Milner, M. (1957). *On Not Being Able to Paint*. New York: International University Press.

Price, L. (1956). *Dialogues of Alfred North Whitehead*. New York: Mentor Books.

Plato. (1965). *Timaeus and Critias.* Translated by D. Lee. London: Penguin.
Poincaré, H. (1952). *Science and Method.* New York: Dover Publications.
Whitehead, A. N. (1929). *Process and Reality.* Corrected ed., D. R. Griffin and D. W. Sherburne, Eds. New York: The Free Press, 1985.
Winnicott, D. W. (1971). *Playing and Reality.* London: Pelican Books.

Chapter 3

Bion's Theory of Thinking

Absence. Container/Contained. Projective
Identification and Hallucination

Introduction

In this chapter I examine Bion's (1962) theory of thinking which, as
with Plato's *Timaeus*, emerges out of awareness of absence, and the
interplay between container–contained and paranoid–schizoid and
depressive position. Projective identification is conceptualized by Bion
as the process of transformation and the origin of the capacity to
think. He differentiates the psychotic and non-psychotic parts of the
personality in order to understand the potential of normal hallucination for growth and the detrimental effect of pathological mentation.

Bion's Theory of Thinking and its Relation to Absence

For Bion too, thoughts/thinking emerge out of absence. He depicted
the first thoughts which he called *Beta-elements*, as compounded of
things-in-themselves, feelings of depression – persecution and guilt and
therefore aspects of the personality linked to a sense of catastrophe.

Bion posited that first thoughts or beta-elements are indistinguishable
from body sensations and outer objects. They constitute the hallucinatory
raw material, which must be worked through in order to become part of a
thinking process. They feel catastrophic because the mind has no frame of
reference for them. What is catastrophic is the break-up or loss of a prior
goodness (or imagined, longed-for-goodness) – 'What it was there yesterday …' in Plato's *Timaeus* (1965), or what Winnicott (1949) calls the
'discontinuity of going on being'.

In 1935, Bion attended Jung's *Tavistock Lectures*. The fifth lecture in
particular seems to have had the most important impact on Bion, in
the sense that Jung had elaborated there on themes which will appear

DOI: 10.4324/9781003261841-4

again quite centrally in Bion's working model of the container and in his version of projective identification. The first hint of container and contained in Bion's work, though not yet in the sense of the container–contained model, appeared when Bion relates that in the fantasy of a schizophrenic patient the expelled particles of the ego lead an independent and uncontrolled existence outside the personality (Bion, 1956), where they can either contain external objects or are contained by them. Bion achieved the first formulation of his complete model/ formulation of container–contained six years later in *Learning from Experience*, which appeared in the year following Jung's death (Bion, 1962). Here Bion's model of the living container, which, together with the content it has taken into itself, continues to develop.

If for Jung the archetype of container–contained is the alchemical relationship of patient–analyst, that is, their *coniunctio*, for Bion the archetype of container–contained is mother's breast–infant. An infant in pain (patient's mind) is searching and being found by the mother's breast (analyst's mind). For Winnicott (1963), the individual takes delight in hiding, but feels devastated if he/she is not found.

If for Jung the mind is composed of opposites, similarly, Bion's conceptualization is that the personality is constituted out of dual elements: container–contained. There may also be a realization contained seeking a container; thoughts without a thinker. In the same way that transference is forever in search of a container. For Bion, the mating, the seeking completion is conceptualized thus: the pre-conception is open to, and searching for, a particular experience with which it can match up and then be complete. This mating renders it emotionally real and is associated with the subjective experience of realizing something, that is, understanding its meaning – a conception is born.

Some pre-conceptions may be innate, or archetypal, for example, an infant seems to search for something on which it can suck, as though it has an in-built idea about something like a breast that is available and can satisfy its needs. Bion (1962) says that there is no limit to the number of realizations which can satisfy an innate pre-conception. Having become a conception, a new pre-conception is ready to mate. This whole process is that of thoughts growing in complexity and depth.

Bion realized that the Oedipus myth was important not only for the content of its phantasies, but also for the development of the apparatus of thinking. For example, the announcement by the Oracle about the projected tragedy can be defined as what Bion calls a 'definitory hypothesis', that is, a definition of the patient's state of mind. Tireseus, the seer's advice against Oedipus's wish to pursue the truth could be seen as the element opposed to the emergence of truth. Oedipus, in his attempt to enquire into the cause of the plague, heedless of warnings against this, can be thought of as an inquiry and probing. Expulsion from Thebes involves action, rather than thought. The Sphinx scrutinizes, asks questions and stimulates curiosity, but also threatens death if it is not answered satisfactorily.

For Bion, as for Jung, the relationship (mother–infant or patient–therapist) is absolutely vital, and how each participant is affected and changed by it. Their language, however, is different; while Jung speaks of projection and empathy as the alchemical process of transformation, Bion speaks of projective identification.

The concept of projective identification was first formulated by Melanie Klein in one of her seminal papers: *Notes on some Schizoid Mechanisms*, 1946. It is usually the revised edition of 1952 which Bion actually cites.

For Melanie Klein, projective identification referred to the operation of a grandiose phantasy which serves to defend against primitive anxieties. Bion (1959) extended the concept of projective identification by showing how it is the vital dynamic between patient and analyst, as well as groups of all types, that is of the utmost importance. By doing so, Bion developed the concept of projective identification from being understood as an intrapsychic event only, to being both an intrapsychic event and interpersonal phenomenon, in addition to being an important means of communication. In other words, with his studies of containment – container–contained – Bion added a further dimension to the concept of projective identification, now taking into account the reaction of the mother–therapist to her baby's–patient's projective identification. Bion (1959, 1962) described the mother's role, which is so significant to child development, as that of taking the infant's unbearable anxieties and being affected by its psychic distress.

Bion (1962) says that from Klein's theory of projective identification he shall abstract for use as a model the idea of a container into which an object is projected, and the object that can be projected into the container which he designates by the term contained. For him, emotion flows between container and contained, binding them together. Thus conjoined or permeated or both they change in a manner usually described as growth.

Projective identification consists in the omnipotent phantasy that the unwanted parts of the personality and internal objects (people, and internalized relationships to significant other/others, aspects of oneself) can be disowned, projected and controlled in the object into which they have been projected. Projective identification is used not only to evacuate bad feelings/aspects of oneself, that is, for relieving the ego of bad parts, but also for preserving good parts by protecting them from a bad internal world, for attacking and destroying the object, etc. This mechanism, which according to Klein and Bion, is part of the primitive defences used in the first few months of life, acquires a different modality of functioning during the transition from the paranoid–schizoid position to the depressive position. The normal function of the projective identification constitutes one of the main factors in symbol formation and human communication, and determines a relationship of empathy with the object, providing the possibility of putting oneself in someone else's place/shoes and, in so doing, to understand his/her feelings better. Bion attaches great importance to this mechanism and considers it the origin of an activity that will later be described as the capacity to think. But for this process to take place, a container, a good breast, or an understanding object is necessary; one that is capable of receiving the bad parts, phantasies and feelings of the infant, and modifying them by thought – reverie – and giving them back to the infant, so that he can re-introject them in a more tolerable form.

Whether one wishes to call it reverie, free-floating attention, alphafunction, container, receptacle, the state of mind of the analyst, their anticipatory state, their pre-conception, the important fact is that the therapist needs to be in a maximally receptive state, in order to be open to the particular experience of the session. Thus, Bion's idea is of the need for the analyst in each session to get rid of memory and desire, in order to be open to the new experience of the day. This, of course, is a paradoxical situation to be in, for memory and desire are part of what makes us human, in other words, we cannot depart from our humanity. What is more, the therapist is both in an anticipatory state of mind, and, simultaneously, trying not to be blinded by memory and desire. Perhaps what matters most is that he is able to maintain the tension and try not to be obfuscated by memory and desire, while recognizing that his anticipatory state includes a desire for something, even if the something is not clearly defined or known. One has some idea, though, in that what one is expectant of is the new experience itself – whatever that might be.

In essence, what Bion, based on Klein's notion of projective identification, is saying, is that in absence, that is, through the experience of absence, psychotic anxieties and primitive defence mechanisms are activated in adult life, or rather, re-activated; and how the patient must establish contact with his emotional life, which poses the dilemma of evolution and differentiation, and of having to face the fears associated with this evolution.

As Jung had anticipated, the psychological birth of the Self is a terrifying prospect. Sessions are intensively charged with emotions. The underlying emotional impulses might be so strong that the individual will tend to activate omnipotent phantasies in order to avoid the frustration in learning from experience, when learning implies effort, pain and contact with reality. Yet, growth, as Jung so clearly understood, can only come from suffering, that is, it can only come about through conflict, disorganization, pain and frustration. On the other hand, when this does not happen, that is, when the infant or the patient cannot tolerate absence and its accompanying unbearable feelings, a form of pathological projective identification takes place. This pathological organization, according to Bion, takes place in certain psychotic illnesses and it is used by the psychotic personality, as well as by the psychotic part of the personality in every one of us, where there is a predominance of envy and greed. In this case, the splitting of parts of the ego is so severe that it results in a multiplicity of minute fragments which are violently projected into the object. These fragments create a reality populated by bizarre objects, which become increasingly painful and persecuting. The consequence of this is a further increase in projective identification, that is, further pathological splitting and projection which, in turn, increasingly damages the perceptual and judging apparatus, and results in further withdrawal from reality.

The term 'bizarre objects' was created by Bion to describe the kind of objects by which the psychotic patient feels surrounded. Through pathological splitting and projective identification he tries to rid himself not only of the object, but also and deliberately of all the ego functions connected with the incipient reality principle (primitive thoughts, consciousness, attention, judgement), especially of those elements that have a linking function.

In the patient's belief, the particles of ego function that are fragmented and violently evacuated penetrate and occupy the real objects and engulf them. In turn, the engulfed object attacks the projected part of the personality and strips it of vitality. This results in a bizarre object, composed of a part of the personality and parts of the object, in a relation of container–contained that strips both of vitality.

In terms of the theory of development of thought, the bizarre object is formed by beta-elements, residues of the ego, of the superego, and of external objects. The attempt to use these elements for thinking makes him take primitive thoughts for real objects and he feels confused. The psychotic part of the personality places in the real world what the non-psychotic part/person represses and, as a consequence, his unconscious seems to have been replaced by a world of bizarre objects. Bion points out that this world of bizarre objects is not a world of dream. In other words, the individual feels locked up in this world, and must use these bizarre objects instead of using what for the non-psychotic personality (or non-psychotic part of the personality) would be thoughts. He gets imprisoned in the claustrum, as opposed to being able to think, which, in turn, will enable tolerance of absence and doubt, and a sense of the infinite. In this situation, the container–contained is absent (minus container–contained), and there is a tendency to organize a 'super' ego that is in omniscient opposition to learning from experience; this is an affirmation of destructive superiority, a determination to possess, in order to stop what is possessed from having an existence of its own. This provokes guilt feelings which are extremely persecutory. The attacked returns with a vengeance, so to speak.

For Bion, it is crucial to differentiate the psychotic from the non-psychotic parts of the personality, in order to understand both the potential of normal hallucination for consciousness, thinking, feeling real, and to continue to grow in imaginative ways, and the detrimental effect of pathological hallucination, where one's own inner world and world at large can only feel like a frightening and dangerous place to inhabit.

One may ask: Is this division of the personality as psychotic and non-psychotic useful, or is it another oversimplification and fallacy of misplaced concreteness? Like anything else in the mind it can be both. But the fact remains: What makes some of us, or part of us so destructive towards ourselves, our objects, others, the world, that we destroy our own matrix for thinking and ourselves in the process? It seems that one must consider both a congenial disposition, as well as the relationship with a mother who was unable to perform her function of receiving, containing and modifying the violent emotions projected by the child. In other words, one needs to look for an originally defective container within, and an external lack of containment and container.

The clinical transference manifestations of the defences of absence include attack on linking of incipient thoughts, as well as the links of sense–perceptions, together with their consciousness. The patient (unconsciously) tries to dissociate his own mind, as well as the mind of the therapist, and obstructs understanding, for any progress confronts him with the pain of getting to know 'madness'. Arrogance, pathological hallucinations, forced splitting, etc., are also part of the picture in which therapists find themselves caught up on behalf of their patients.

Freud (1911) established the evacuative origin of thought, pointing out that it provides a means of restricting motor discharge, and of relieving the increase of tension produced by delaying such discharge. For Freud, it is probable that thinking was originally unconscious, in so far as it went beyond mere ideational representations, and was directed to the relations between impressions of objects, and that it did not acquire further qualities perceptible to consciousness until it became connected with verbal residues. For him, the beginning of dominance of the reality principle goes hand in hand with the development of an ability to think and thus bridge the frustrating gap between the moment a need is felt and the point at which appropriate action satisfies it. In other words, by 1911 Freud was already positing that thinking develops out of absence, out of the need to bridge the gap between absence and satisfaction.

Bion reformulated the existing theories about the process of thinking. For him, 'thinking' is a function of the personality which arises from the interaction of a variety of factors – he proposed a theory of functions. Alpha-function, in particular, enabled Bion to study and understand the capacity to think, as well as disturbances of thought.

The theory of alpha-function postulates the existence of a function of the personality – alpha-function – which operates on sense impressions and on perceived emotional experiences, transforming them into alpha-elements. These, unlike the perceived impressions, can be used in new processes of transformation, for storing, for depression, etc. Alpha-elements are then, those sense perceptions and emotional experiences transformed into a visual, auditory, olfactory, or other images in the mental domain. They are used in the formation of dream–thoughts, unconscious thinking during wakefulness, dreams and memories. Bion calls beta-elements those sense impressions and emotional experiences that are not transformed. These elements are not appropriate for thinking, dreaming, remembering, or exercising intellectual functions usually related to the psychic apparatus. These elements are experienced as things-in-themselves (Kant, 1781) and are generally evacuated through projective identification.

The theory of thought formulated by Bion starts by proposing that thoughts are prior to thinking. In other words, that thoughts exist and give rise to an apparatus for manipulating them called thinking – thinking as the container for thoughts. Even though in the earlier stages of development, thoughts, in agreement with Freud, might not be but mere sense impressions and very primitive emotional experiences (proto-thoughts) related to the concrete experience of a thing-in-itself (as Kant defines the unknowable in the object), and, thinking, a way of unburdening the psyche of excessive and overwhelming stimulus.

When using the term 'thought', Bion refers to thoughts, pre-conceptions, conceptions, thoughts proper and concepts. Bion's theory of thinking can be roughly outlined thus: for the baby, the taking of milk, warmth and love are equated with incorporating a good breast. He assumes that although the baby has an innate pre-conception of the breast, he is not, however, aware of its need for the good breast. Driven by hunger, it experiences an unsatisfied need (the bad breast or the non-breast) which it tries to get rid of. The experience of absence becomes a bad presence. For Bion, all needed objects are bad objects; they are needed because they are not possessed, otherwise there will be no deprivation. Therefore, the primitive thoughts or proto-thoughts are bad objects the baby needs to get rid of. The real experience with the actual breast provides the baby the opportunity to get rid of this bad breast. The mother provides not only food, but is the container for all the unpleasant feelings (bad breast) of the baby. The elimination of the bad breast into the mother constitutes the elimination of a beta-element through the mechanism of projective identification. In terms of the theory of thought, Bion suggests that, in this case, one has a complex situation. On the one hand, one can say that a pre-conception (innate expectation of the breast analogous to Kant's concept of 'empty thought', or Jung's Archetype, or Platonic Forms) has mated with a realization (real experience with the breast) giving birth to a conception. When the pre-conception is not found in the real breast there is a combination of a pre-conception and a frustration – a situation which Bion calls negative realization, which can give rise to the appearance of 'thought'.

Although tolerance of frustration appears to be an innate factor in the baby's personality, the unpleasant non-breast, or absence of breast may not be tolerated long enough to become a thought, that is, if the absence and the feeling experience cannot be thought, then, the tendency will be to expel it, but one is left with a bad figure which acts. The therapist sees in his practice patients who instead of being able to think and bear the thought of absence, act, by clinging to paranoid feelings or to self-punishment. Rejection of absence, rejection of painful feelings, refusal to think, blocks the development of thought and thinking about the Self, and one remains stuck in a vicious cycle.

In general, projection (including evacuatory projection) refuses to think and yet, without projection no unconscious content can be understood.

Since these defence mechanisms when dealing with absence, pain and frustration are shared by all of us, and although their persistence, severity and intensity is what marks the difference in one's experience, perhaps it is safe to say that some of us live in the claustrum temporarily and others permanently.

In Bion's theory of thinking, thinking designates two processes that are actually different; a recipient and a percipient form of thinking. The former refers to 'thoughts without a thinker', that is, thoughts 'waiting' for a thinker to think them. The latter refers to the development of thoughts within the personality. In other words, sometimes one needs to think thoughts through, and struggle with them, and other times a thought presents to one as if out of the blue – as a revelation.

According to Bion, two main mechanisms take part in the formation of the apparatus for thinking thoughts; the first is represented by the dynamic relation of container–contained, and the second by that of the paranoid–schizoid and depressive position. At first, if all goes well, the baby repeatedly internalizes good experiences of its relation with the mother. This means that the baby has internalized a 'happy couple' formed by a receptive and metabolizing mother (container), through the alpha-function of the feelings projected by the baby, and by the baby who, through projective identification, has placed his/her various emotions (contained) in her. The mother who functions as an effective container of the infant's sensations can successfully transform hunger into satisfaction, pain into pleasure, loneliness into company, fear of dying (the 'nameless dread') into peacefulness. This capacity of the mother to be open to the baby's projected need is her capacity for reverie.

Regarding the second mechanism, that of the dynamic interaction between the paranoid–schizoid position and the depressive position, it refers to the tolerance of moments of disintegration and integration. Bion cites what Poincaré (1952) described as the discovery of the 'selected fact'. A selected fact is an emotion or an idea which gives coherence to what is dispersed and introduces order into disorder.

For Bion, in the formation and use of thoughts, as in the integration of the object, both processes – container–contained and paranoid-schizoid/depressive position – operate together and one cannot ascribe more importance to one than the other. In other words, the linking, which is the essence of thinking, is itself brought about by the linking of two processes, inasmuch as the development of thought and thinking depends on the interplay of two fundamental groups of factors – innate tolerance or intolerance of absence and frustration, and environmental factors, that is, the mother's capacity for reverie.

By advocating that psychotherapists approach the work, the task of observation, exploration and experience without memory or desire, Bion is advocating the need for uncertainty which, in turn, increases creativity, and the development of intuition, enabling the therapist to get into a state of reverie, or a state of self-discovery. But, for this to happen, the therapist himself needs to be able to tolerate absence and frustration, as well as his own discoveries constantly transforming and expanding through his relationship with patients. The therapist needs to tolerate the paradoxical nature of the work, in between and beyond uniqueness and generalization.

For Freud (1900), hallucinatory phenomena in the infant/patient are the result of his tendency to satisfy a desire in the absence of the gratifying object. He calls this, hallucinatory realization of desires under the dominance of the pleasure principle. When in normal development the infant's ego is faced with evidence that the hallucinatory realization of desires does not provide appropriate satisfaction, it will give up this method and replace it with others which are more realistic and use thoughts under the dominance of the reality principle.

For Freud, the capacity to hallucinate is universal, and can be normal and pathological. He believes that the persistence of this hallucinatory function of the psychic apparatus can be found in dream phenomena and in psychotic illness, which he partially explains as a regression to this primitive method of functioning. Not only does every individual create hallucinatory phenomena in his dreams, but also the types of thought processes that create dreams also go on while he is awake. In other words, there is reason to believe that the way the individual construes his world has hallucinatory aspects. In that sense, the ability to produce a hallucinatory state seems part and parcel of human ability to produce images and words. Most people, whether palatable or not, seem to have psychotic, neurotic and realistic inner voices.

Freud, Klein and Winnicott believed that human infants must pass through a phase of 'normal psychosis' – where the mechanisms for dealing with the impact of internal and external reality include: dissociation, denial, omnipotence, idealization, projective identification, denigration, splitting, etc. – which will later be outgrown and, simultaneously, will be present for life, and re-emerge at times of difficulty.

For Bion, however, hallucinations and dream–thoughts are different. While the hallucinations are the evacuation of beta-elements and correspond therefore to a primitive mental level of functioning, dream–thoughts represent a higher level of functioning characterized by the presence of alpha-elements. He conceptualizes hallucinatory phenomena as different from dreams, and attributes the former to the psychotic part of the personality. What Bion is pointing out is that the plasticity of the infant is not available to the psychotic personality, which becomes rigid. That is, while the infant passes through many stages in the course of a profoundly orderly developmental unfolding, and perceptual, cognitive and fantastical dimensions have their timetables, by contrast, the psychotic's timetable seems to have gone awry, and broad possibilities of experience have been closed off.

One may find oneself partially agreeing with both views: Freud's and Bion's, in that there seems to be such a rigid quality in some of the narratives of patients, and yet, it is this hallucinatory quality that often opens up into unforeseen possibilities. By the same token, that thing one calls 'reality' is imbued with much more hallucination than any one would like to admit. For example, day-dreams, desires, plans, visions, expectations, daily existence is hallucination, and hallucination one's reality.

For Kant (1781), desire is an act of imagination and creation and not the response to a lack. It is an active and autonomous power of the mind which conjures up the object of desire and not the other way around. Thus, desire cannot be understood in terms of negativity and absence.

In opposition, for Lacan, desire is lack. Whitehead agrees with Kant, in that desire is not a lack, but rather what the subject imagines and creates. However, he does not place the subject, as Kant does, at the beginning of the productive system of desire, but at the end. For Whitehead (1929, p. 29), the subject is always also a superject, coming after the process of creation rather than before, and experiencing "satisfaction" (Ibid., pp. 25–26), or "self-enjoyment" (Ibid., pp. 145, 289), precisely to the extent that it is itself a product of this satisfaction. For Whitehead, this inversion implies a movement from the world to the Self (rather than as in Kant, from the Self to the world), and implicitly privileges passion, disinterest over desire.

For Whitehead, desire and aesthetic feeling mobilize the will and the soul, and transform the Self and the world. In other words, through desire the Self projects itself into the world and transforms it, and through aesthetic feeling the world projects itself into the Self procuring its transformation.

The original sense of 'desiderare' from the Latin is 'to wait for what the stars will bring', and this is part of the desiring and hallucinatory beings we all are. According to Bion, transformations in hallucination are correlated with a primitive 'disaster' or 'catastrophe', in which the emotional contents, things-in-themselves, beta-elements, have not found a container (mother with reverie) to contain and transform them – the 'nameless dread' that is returned to the infant under these conditions, or 'psychotic panic', constitute a mode of mental functioning in an area of infinite dimensions that cannot act as a container. In this state the psychotic personality adopts defences geared to avoid panic by evacuating the functions which would be capable of the experience. The primitive catastrophe is transformed. Hallucinations, actions or words are used for evacuation, that is, acting out, which includes self-denigration and a severe sense of guilt.

The person that uses this type of transformation believes that his 'reactions' are the result of his capacity to surround himself by a universe generated by himself to provide an 'infallible' method of avoiding the pain of frustration. The person 'believes' that his method is superior to any other method that is proposed to him as help, especially the method proposed by psychoanalysis. This can also be formulated as 'complete freedom from the restriction imposed by reality', because there is no such reality: the 'reality' is the transformation in hallucinosis.

Winnicott (1969) makes another important contribution when he says that behind a neurosis may be a hidden psychosis.

Mr. H., an intelligent and functional man in the external world, is convinced that the entire world is against him, that he has been born under a dark star, and that no matter what he does to ameliorate his situation, his doomed fate will always take the upper hand. He feels superior to his friends and family – from most of whom he is now estranged – and sustains a deep belief that he is better than anyone else. He feels resentful that all these 'lesser people' with low moral standards, diminished intelligence and lack of aesthetic capacity have a more fulfilled life than himself, but he is adamant that he is a 'truer being'. In our sessions, he often discusses the 'delusions' of his acquaintances, and I often point out his own delusions and hallucinations in rationality, but invariably he gets irritated by what seems to him as my attempt to destroy his invincible and superior method of being and thinking. When, on occasions, he is able to reflect on his own predicament, then, the pendulum swings back onto a vicious attack on himself: a denigratory attitude and a concomitant severe feeling of guilt ensues, for what he does to others and to himself. At face value, one could not envisage the intricate system, one which has been built in order to protect himself from the pain of absence and isolation he lives in.

A system of hallucinosis is thus based on the intolerance of the absence of the object with the concomitant intolerance of the pain of frustration. According to Bion, the evacuation of beta-elements creates the 'domain of the non-existent', a mental world where what is non-existent 'exists', and therefore what does not exist is the painful suffering of frustration. The gratification of 'freedom' provided by this system of hallucinosis is, from the point of view of the observer who uses (mostly) transformations in thought, a 'freedom' that is really an enclosure and a restriction, that is, a claustrum. But from the point of view of the psychotic part of the personality, 'freedom' resides in the immediacy of the result, without being 'limited' by the creation of symbols, words, dreams or other manifestations which have the quality of representing something.

The transformation in hallucinosis is a particular form of functioning of the psychotic area of the personality and creates a space occupied by non-existent objects. 'Is' indicates that something is not. Absence is not allowed to be filled with bad presences, that is, with frustration, and yet, this is precisely what happens, in that it may not be filled with frustration and the pain of absence, but it is filled with persecutory presences. This is the way that this precarious system backfires. The patient's state of mind is that he can be self-supporting because he can hallucinate everything he needs; he can get all the mental and physical sustenance it requires. But, in reality, he cannot get that sustenance from the evacuated objects, that is, from his hallucinations, leaving him deprived and impoverished, while the psychotherapist can feel superior about his own method and cleverness. But the patient remains convinced that his hallucinations are real and superior.

Mr. F. fears that through psychoanalytic treatment, the therapist will remove his stoicism which he most values. An artist fears losing his creativity through therapy. Both participants – patient and therapist – experience the strong rivalry between transformations in hallucinosis and transformation through psychoanalysis. The transformation in hallucinosis of the patient and the transformation in psychoanalysis appear at times to be in competition with each other.

Miss P. arrived for her session and announced that it would be her last session, since her vision of the world and herself in it is incompatible with mine. She says she knows herself well and cannot comprehend what the psychoanalytic method is about. We managed to discuss her sense of rivalry with her siblings, boyfriend and myself, as well as her competition for the love of her parents, in addition to her intolerance of not being able to control our process; emotions and unpredictable thoughts 'intrude' into our sessions, to her annoyance. Our conversation led to her staying in therapy, at least for the time being. I say it cautiously because, in agreement with Bion, although the disagreement/rivalry has been made conscious, it still continues to exist. It is only that now it has become endo-psychic, that is, the rival methods struggle for supremacy within the patient. This is a sign of progress but, simultaneously, it produces further difficulties. For example, the characteristics of the conflict are easier to discern when externalized as a conflict between analyst and patient and this can lead to collusion between the two, for the patient finds it more bearable and the analyst easier. What is more, any benefit achieved as a result of the analytic process can be vitiated by its being indistinguishable from 'defect' of the patient, and any victory of the patient is vitiated by perpetuating the painful status quo.

Mr. H. both punishes himself for his 'defective' and 'immoral' character and often states that he is in a 'no-win' situation. And I think that he is partly right, but for different reasons. What I mean is that a capacity for compassion on the part of the therapist is a source of admiration and, consequently, of envy in the patient who feels incapable of mature compassion. At this point, as perhaps throughout any psychoanalytic treatment, it is the relationship that matters the most. That is to say, the crux is found in the character of the cooperation between the two people and not in the problem for which cooperation is required.

The nature of the cooperation may be determined by the disturbances of the personality of the patient, but that situation may be presumed to be amenable to psychoanalysis; it differs from the situation produced by the inborn disposition of the patient. According to Bion, if analysis has been successful in restoring the personality of the patient, he will approximate to being the person he was when his development became compromised. One could view this as a sweeping statement which sounds good in principle, but which one does not know what it means. To start with, one may find it impossible to decide whether an attitude is inborn, or made necessary by environmental circumstances. All one can observe is its intensity, severity and frequency. Secondly, some of the stubbornness to change seems to have not only a personal quality, but also an archetypal one. Thirdly, most patients fear that in the search for their real Self/personality, or in the depths of it, they will find that there is 'nothing' to discover, in the sense that they will either dissolve into nothingness or encounter an alienated Self. There is another aspect that also feels inseparable, which is that the patient's well-being and vitality spring from the same characteristics which give trouble and thus, it can go either way. The sense that loss of the bad parts of his personality is inseparable from loss of that part in which all his mental well-being resides contributes to the acuity of the patient's fears.

Although we may believe that the term 'hallucination' or 'transformation in hallucinosis' describes adequately the state of mind we are attempting to describe, we may wonder if we are pathologizing it by calling it so, and whether they would not be best reserved for extreme states of mind where contact with reality has been completely (or almost completely) severed. But, if not hallucination, what would be a better term for it? One could settle for contrivance.

The container, the receptacle, the alpha-function of the therapist clarifies emotion and detoxifies it, that is, it has the function of the nurse of all becoming and change (Plato's *Timaeus*, 1965). This process, of course, depends on the container being able to contain the emotion. But, as Bion (1965) points out, it can go that way, but it may also be a container not able to tolerate the emotion, and the contained emotion may not be able to tolerate neglect. This results in what Bion calls 'hyperbole'. What this means is that the emotion that cannot tolerate neglect grows in intensity, is exaggerated to ensure attention, to enlist the aid of the container, and the container reacts by more, and still more, violent evacuation. The increasing force of emotion produces an increasing force of evacuation which takes the form of either idealizing or denigrating, that is, polarizing and intensifying the opposites, including the opposites of presence/absence, now and not now, here and not here. This refers not so much to the failure of the (external) container to contain, but the lack of container within the patient's experience. There is a failure of realistic projective identification and what occurs instead is an 'explosive projection' – it does not accept the formation of symbols. The patient feels his emotions getting lost in an infinite vacuum. In this mental state of hallucinosis/contrivance, words, images and ideas are debris, or fragments floating in space without limits, or else they may conglomerate and attempt to occupy the place where the object should be. As a result, space and time too can either be integrated or destroyed.

As mentioned above, Bion speaks of a situation where the container is unable to contain, and the contained emotion is not able to tolerate neglect. However, this begs the question: is a container a container if it is not able to contain?, and, is a contained emotion really contained if unable to tolerate neglect?

Bion's Theory of Knowing

Bion's theory of thought and thinking is also a theory about knowing, about learning from and for experience and its disturbances. For Bion all knowledge has its origin in primitive emotional experiences related to the absent object. In other words, all knowledge, inasmuch as all thinking emerges from absence.

In the Kantian sense of the term, Bion assumes that the ultimate reality of the object is unknowable. The object of knowledge of psychoanalysis is one's own or another person's psychic reality (whatever that might mean, since we do not know what psyche or psychic reality is). Through the psychoanalytic process, the therapist attempts to detect these psychoanalytic objects and, through successive abstractions and transformations he tries to find a way of communicating the nature of these objects. For Bion, this process of intuition, abstraction and transformation is similar in some of its characteristics to the process of discovery and abstraction taking place in the infant's mind during development. Thanks to his alpha-function (and his mother's) during this developmental process, the personality comes across the problem of bearing the frustration inherent in the experience Bion calls 'K link' – knowledge. The K link describes the emotional experience that is ever present when two people or two parts of a person are related to each other. Bion selects three of these emotions: Love (L), Hate (H) and Knowledge (K), as intrinsic to the link between two objects, as the requisite for the existence of a relationship. Transference itself is an analytic term implying a relationship between two elements.

Analogous to the pre-conception, the K link refers to an expectation of knowing something which has not as yet been realized. Using the container–contained model, it suggests that a relationship between two elements exists on an emotional background of tolerated doubt.

The attitude called knowing is the activity by which the subject becomes aware of the emotional experience and can abstract from it a formulation which adequately represents that experience. The process of abstraction (in agreement with Whitehead's view) is for Bion essential to the emotional experience of the K link – that linkage present when one is in the process of getting to know the other in an emotional sense, and which involves pain, frustration and loneliness – because the abstracted elements can be used for learning from experience and for understanding. This process, as earlier on described in relationship to thinking, is carried out by the relationship between container and contained and the dynamic interaction between the paranoid–schizoid and the depressive position – integration and disintegration. But, having a piece of knowledge about oneself is not at all the same as getting to know oneself through experiencing these aspects of the Self in relationship to the therapist. What is more, like anything else in psychic life, possession of knowledge can be employed for further discoveries, or to evade the painful experience. Knowing is an emotional experience and what triggers the emotional experience cannot be conceived in isolation from a relationship. The psychoanalytic aim is, through relating, to be able to feel the experience, to think it and to know it. And yet, being able to feel, to think, to know and to formulate the experience is also an entrapment. One cannot help but be trapped in language to such a degree that every attempt to formulate insight is a play on words. This is another example of Whitehead's notion of the fallacy of misplaced concreteness.

Stimulated curiosity searches for knowledge, intolerance of absence and pain, and fear of the unknown stimulate actions and reactions which tend to avoid, cancel out or neutralize the search and the curiosity. This amounts to a resistance which opposes the discovery of new truths. As mentioned previously, Oedipus's curiosity about himself is exemplified throughout the myth, and is epitomized by the riddle of the Sphinx. However, the challenge resides in the arrogant and obstinate manner in which Oedipus carries out his investigation despite the warnings of Tiresias, and the punishment consists of blindness and exile. But it would be wrong to dismiss Oedipus as arrogant and nothing else, in his search. He is taking a risk in exploring and finding out, even if greed for gain is also involved. He undergoes fear, terror, guilt, shame and persecution of risking stirring up frightening ghosts from the past, present and future and, in that respect, he is motivated by a human need to know. What motivates someone to take the risk of exploring themselves, and others to turn a blind eye, or to turn their back on life, remains an open question.

The difference between Freud and Bion lies in motivation; while Freud claimed that the reality principle enabled postponement of immediate gratification, in order to obtain a greater pleasure later on, Bion believed that the motivation lies in the possibility of emotional growth. Whereas Freud saw thought and knowledge as a means of reducing tension, Bion saw it as a means of managing tension.

One may wonder what motivates therapists to get to know themselves and their patients. The motivation is not just about knowing, but also about searching for truth and beauty. In Diotima's words (*Symposium*), all men are bringing to birth in their bodies and their souls … The object which they have in view is birth in beauty. For Whitehead (1929, p. 21), "the many become one, and are increased by one" and through this process creativity achieves its supreme task of transformation into beauty. This concrescent unity is what the poet John Donne (1624) called the 'Emergent Occasion' in its dilemmatic opening to experiential knowledge. It may be conjectured that Plato, Whitehead, Jung, Bion, Winnicott, Freud, etc., developed a profound knowledge of human beings, through a knowledge of their own souls, while keeping the mystery alive. Jung and Bion were not afraid to work with patients on the more psychotic side of the spectrum. Jung, in particular, was deeply in touch with his own psychotic core and went to the depths of his being in his encounter with the unconscious where he met the elderly Elijah and the blind Salome. He had conversations with Philemon – a mythical figure – and was deeply engaged in drawing mandalas, and attempting to understand the hidden meaning in them about his own evolving Self.

In the apparent calm of the consulting room, the therapist too faces the evolution and emergence of the most primitive parts of the mind. What is not, the absence, the void, provides the matrix, or the receptacle from which phenomena appear. The mutual unconsciousness produces psychic and/or physical phenomena which, prior to that were undifferentiated and, invariably, envelops both participants with fear, awe and inspiration.

Controversies between Jung's and Bion's Container Concept

Here I explore some of the criticisms of Jung's container concept in favour of Bion's container. Whilst appreciating Bion's contribution, I defend Jung's container against these critics.

Some have argued that it was Jung who first described very clearly the projection of affects into the analyst, affects that continue to be active there. In the *Tavistock Lectures*, he mentioned the need for (psychotic) patients to find a container of the rejected parts of themselves. But these critics argue that the idea of linking these two elements of theory – namely that the analyst must become a container so that the digested psychic elements can be re-introjected by the patient in a different form – is first reached by Bion. In other words, many psychoanalysts have argued that it is Bion with his theory of transformation and container–contained who hits exactly on the psychodynamic point that makes the greatest emotional demand on the analyst. However, without underestimating Bion's ideas, one may fully disagree with this view, and believe that this crucial notion runs through the entire writings of Jung. Jung is clear in his view: "in the transference analyst and analysand are both altered" (1946, para. 358).

In the fifth of his *Tavistock Lectures* (1935), Jung does not use the term projective identification, but he describes processes that bear a striking resemblance to Bion's later concept. Jung speaks of the concept of projection which is played out in the transference relationship. Transference is a special form of projection which is distinguished by the capacity to place subjective contents unconsciously 'into the object'. Jung (1935) proposes that subjective contents are projected into the object and, thus, they no longer seem to belong to the subject, but instead are found in the other.

Jung (1946, para. 361) states:

> Transference, strictly, … is something which happens between two
> individuals and which, as a rule, is of an emotional and compulsory
> nature. Emotions in themselves are always in some degree over-
> whelming for the subject, because they are involuntary conditions.
> Yet this involuntary condition of the subject is at the same time pro-
> jected into the object, and through that, a bond is established which
> cannot be broken, and exercises a compulsory influence upon the
> subject.

Jung goes further than describing the psychic process as an interpersonal phenomenon, describing how the patient's emotions are
contagious, and how the analyst is 'affected' by the emotions projected into him. The psychic process that Jung is describing corresponds in all essential aspects to the concept of projective
identification that much later Bion describes, and to the notion of
container–contained. Moreover, Jung also applies these psychodynamic insights to the phenomenon of countertransference. Jung
(Ibid., para. 322) describes this psychic infection thus:

> The emotions of patients are always slightly contagious, and they
> are very contagious when the contents which the patient projects
> into the analyst are identical with the analyst's own unconscious
> contents. Then they both fall into the same dark hole of uncon-
> sciousness, and get into the condition of participation. This is the
> phenomenon which Freud described as countertransference. It
> consists of mutual projecting into each other and being fastened
> together by mutual unconsciousness. Participation … is character-
> istic of primitive psychology, that is, of a psychological level where
> there is no conscious discrimination between subject and object.

Others have criticized Jung's description of events in the transference–
countertransference relationship, which he links to alchemical symbolism, as distant from the affects that determine them. And further, they
claim that nowhere does Jung explicitly describe an interactional container model of the analytic situation; instead, it is always alluded to

merely in a symbolic way, as if Jung was afraid to approach it more directly. The implication of this argument is that clinical data can cause anxiety because it resonates in the analyst's unconscious, breaks through his own repression barrier and thereby has a stimulating effect on his unconscious contents, creating, thereby, anxiety. However, one could argue against this view, by reminding oneself that through his encounters with the unconscious at the risk of a breakdown, as well as in his work with the psychotic aspects of the patient's personality, Jung went all the way into his depths, perhaps much further than most therapists are prepared to go, and that, in risking a real breakdown he gifted us with a breakthrough in our understanding of psyche. One could further argue that by hinting and using symbols, Jung has a higher aim in mind, allowing for the emergent container to emerge, as opposed to putting the lid on it and killing it off with concrete and rationalistic detail. Perhaps all one can say is that both Jung's theory and Bion's are yet another myth, another story like Plato's *Timaeus*, but no less real because of it. Plato was speculating about the emergence/creation of the world, and human beings in it: the beginnings of all beginnings, and so is the therapist, for he is speculating about the beginning of human psychological development, about becoming, existing, thinking, feeling and being, about psyche and psychic reality, that is, about the birth of the Self. And, like Plato, while the work continues, the therapist must constantly remind himself that 'one can only tell the most likely tale'.

References

Bion, W. R. (1956). Development of schizophrenic thoughts. *Second Thoughts.* London: Karnac, 1987.

Bion, W. R. (1959). Attacks on linking. *Second Thoughts.* London: Maresfiled Library/Karnac, 1967.

Bion, W. R. (1962). Learning from experience. *Seven Servants.* New York: Jason Aronson, 1977.

Bion, W. R. (1965). Transformations. *Seven Servants.* New York: Jason Aronson, 1977.

Donne, J. (1624). Devotions upon emergent occasions. *Meditation* XVII. Oxford: Oxford University Press, 1975.

Freud, S. (1900). The interpretation of dreams. *Standard Edition, 4, 5.*

Freud, S. (1911). Formulations of the two principles of mental functioning. *Standard Edition, 12.*

Jung, C. G. (1935). The Tavistock Lectures. *Collected Works*, vol. 18.

Jung, C. G. (1946). *The Psychology of the Transference.* Translated by R. F. C. Hull. London: Routledge, 1983.

Kant, I. (1781). *Critique of Pure Reason.* Trans. W. S. Phumar. Indianapolis: Hackett, 1996.

Klein, M. (1946). Notes on some schizoid mechanisms. *International Journal of Psycho-Analysis*, 27, 99–110, 1952.

Plato. (1951). *The Symposium.* Translated by W. Hamilton. London: Penguin.

Plato. (1965). *Timaeus and Critias.* Translated by D. Lee. London: Penguin.

Poincaré, H. (1952). *Science and Method.* New York: Dover Publications.

Whitehead, A. N. (1929). *Process and Reality.* Corrected ed., D. R. Griffin and D. W. Sherburne, Eds. New York: The Free Press, 1985.

Winnicott, D. W. (1949). Mind and its relation to soma. *British Journal of Medical Psychology*, 27, 201–209.

Winnicott, D. W. (1963). Dependence in infant-care, in childcare, and in the psychoanalytic setting. *The Maturational Process and the Facilitating Environment.* London: Karnac, 1990.

Winnicott, D. W. (1969). The use of an object and relating through identifications. *International Journal of Psycho-Analysis*, 50, 711–716.

Chapter 4

Absence as Precursor to Pathological Organization and Equally as Basic to Psychic Life

Introduction

For Whitehead (1929), every part of a man's history has been re-informed by the creative genius of his own present moment. The present is the immortality of the past. It is where absence in all its creativity reigns. However, the creative moment can be thwarted if containment of absence is itself absent.

In Plato's (1965) *Timaeus*, absence, the missing fourth, is conceived as the very essence of the human condition – absence as the nurse of all becoming and change. Green (1983) emphasizes absence both as basic to human life and as the precursor to pathological organization. Along similar lines, Winnicott defines the transitional object as a 'not-me' possession which is an entrée to discover the normal development both towards psychological well-being, and equally towards pathology. The absence referred to in psychopathology is not one that can be restored or alleviated by the return of the presence, nor is it a loss since it cannot be named. Instead, this absence makes reference to the non-existent which becomes the only thing that is real.

André Green's Views on Absence

In his book *The Dead Mother* Green (1983) is both describing a particular pattern of pathological organization of a child attempting to enliven a depressed, bereft, or absent mother through identification with the object – via compulsive mentation, intense sexual rivalry, auto-erotic retreat, etc. – in order to sustain a precarious link to the depleted other. But, at another level, Green is elaborating his project of theorizing absence as a fundamental property of psychic life.

DOI: 10.4324/9781003261841-5

Absence includes blankness, emptiness, negative narcissism, anxiety, non-breast, non-integration, non-object, nothingness, void, the missing fourth in Plato's *Timaeus*. This latter point made by Green is crucial to the present discussion. This is where it began, in the sense that it is not just about the pathological consequences of absence, but about absence as the very essence of the human condition – absence as the nurse of all becoming and change. In the opening of *Timaeus*, Plato is narrating an ordinary, basic experience/event of someone (or something) missing. This is the person's lot. What is psychoanalysis but an enabling a process of mourning (the Self), often long overdue. A process of mourning and burying the death (within), so that one can be alive.

Freud (1917) states that what is to be forgotten must first be remembered, for remembering is a kind of forgetting – a way of letting go. For Bion, only that which can be forgotten can be used for dream-thoughts. From this perspective, absence is in opposition to the black-and-white space of emptiness, negativity, blank mourning, non-being, nothingness.

Green thinks of the dead mother syndrome/complex as metaphorically analogous to mourning; he makes it clear that the patient is responding not to the mother's loss, but to her bereavement, that is, to her emotional absence in relation to the child. For Green (1983), the essential characteristic of this depression is that it takes place in the presence of the object, which is physically present but emotionally absent, in the sense of being immersed in its own bereavement. It is a response to the mother's deadness. Green writes of the ruination of psyche down to the degree that it cannot be. The subject is encapsulated in a deadened relationship with the object, and it itself becomes deadened as its own vitality and life evaporates. 'To be' becomes forbidden and one's right to exist becomes questionable.

The dead mother, unlike the normal period of the mother's mourning – the typical despair, sadness or frustration which sweeps into the psyche of all mothers, the 'certain hour of maternal sorrow' as Eliot calls it – refuses her own moods, killing off contact with the processes of inner life. But, primary identification with the mother's affective deadness is the most pathological and malignant outcome. Selective forces within the individual come into play that will contribute to resilience or lack of resilience. These include the infant's or child's cognitive capacities, capacity to accept paradox (of the transitional object in Winnicott's terms that is both created from within and presented from outside). If able to recognize similarity and difference from the mother, the effect may not be so damaging. The capacity to create transformative metaphors of life experiences also plays a part. These cognitive traits contribute to the child's faculty for creative fantasy and imagination. What is crucial for some individuals is the ability to construct alternative inner worlds of the imagination that will effectively remove them from the impingement of a traumatizing relationship with the mother. Some individuals will remain open to new experience while others will remain prisoners of the past. Shakespeare (1595/1596) captures it in a *Midsummer Night's Dream*:

> And as imagination bodies
> forth the form of things
> unknown, the poet's pen
> turns them to shapes, and
> gives to aery nothing a
> local habitation and name.

An important aspect of Green's notion of the dead mother is that, like Jung, Bion, Freud and Winnicott, he emphasizes both absence as bad presence, and absence as potential presence. For example, for Green (1986a), absence falls between presence as intrusion and loss as annihilation. And, then, in 1986b, Green speaks of how absence leans towards the potential of presence, rather than towards loss. Once again, in psychological matters, it can go either way.

When Green is describing absence as loss, he speaks of the tendency of the psychic structure to dissolve towards, revolve around, and adhere to nothingness. This negative presence, this absence becomes the gravity of a psychic life founded upon loss.

One hears a patient explicitly and implicitly saying: "all I have got is what I have not got". Absence then becomes the graveyard of the subject, where attacks on linking (negative knowledge (-K, Bion, 1959), unintegration (Winnicott, 1963) or madness (Green, 1983)) reign.

Perhaps the deepest secret of the dead mother is that her impact is always deadening, but she actually never dies. Similarly, John Steiner in *Psychic Retreats* (1993) has written of a half-dead state where both object and Self are tormented, but not allowed to die. This state is a psychic retreat from the full measure of guilt and loss that separation from objects entails. In such a state, it is the agency of the subject – desire, aggression, sex, separateness, life itself – that remains suspended.

On the other hand, Green, like previously Jung, Bion, Winnicott, Plato and others elevates absence to a form of creative structure; for it is out of this structure, which includes the negative hallucination of the mother, that allows for the emergent container to emerge, that is, the subjectivity of the individual with its vital affects and thoughts. For as long as the dead mother is never absent, it occupies a psychic space, so to speak, in which nothing can truly enter or emerge. It is the capacity to bear and endure the absence, as opposed to being anchored/imprisoned in/by absence that breaks the spell of deadly repetition. Only absence allows for new thought and experience.

Green helps us to recognize, as well, that all 'felt thoughts' are both shadow and light, that is, the presence of psychic experience rests on a penumbra of absence. In the lived experience of the analytic relationship 'felt thoughts' and 'thought feelings' can be created between and within each member of the analytic couple. A potential space, an emergent container is born wherein the flow of psychic life may be engaged. At the boundary of Self and Other one risks encountering each other's shadow and light. That is, one takes up the chance of both mutuality and negation of reciprocity, as well as conflict. It is in this risk that the analytic object – inner reality – may potentially be discovered.

Whatever the outcome, one thing seems clear, absence is completely paradoxical and essential. It can get a grip on the person for the worst, it can send him into oblivion, deadness and despair, yet, absence is also a constitutive, creative and necessary condition for a vital and alive psychic life. It is the person's blessing and his curse; the most destructive and the most creative.

The patient's absence, in the sense of missing a session – the missing fourth in Plato's *Timaeus,* or the patient who falls asleep throughout the session, also creates a specific form of psychological effect in the therapist, and in the therapy itself. The analytic process continues despite the patient's physical absence. The specific meanings of the patient's presence in his absence are transformed into analytic objects to be fully experienced, lived with, symbolized, understood and made part of the analytic discourse.

Mr. P. used to sleep through an entire session out of his three weekly sessions. Invariably, while he was fast asleep, my mind will race with day-dreaming images, often of a blissful, if peculiar nature. On one such occasion, I spent the 50 minutes (the duration of the session) riding a horse and galloping through the most improbable and beautiful scenery I have ever seen. Then, I softly woke the patient to announce the end of the session. He got up from the couch, stretched, as from a good night sleep, and thanked me for 'the ride'. In the following session, he remarked on the sense of well-being he had reached in our previous session. He could not quite remember or describe what he had dreamt during the hour, but something to do with the experience of freshness in his face and a sense of freedom. His overwhelming impression was of a positive experience which he would like to access again. To account for this experience of unconscious communication between the patient and myself, I find Winnicott's (1971) notion of the transitional object helpful.

Winnicott's Transitional Object and Its Relation to Green's Views on the Non-existent

Winnicott defines the transitional object as a 'not-me' possession (rather than a need-satisfying-object, an object of desire, or as a fantasized object) which is an entrée to discover the normal development both towards psychological well-being, and equally towards pathology. On the positive side, to distinguish between the first object and the first 'not-me' possession, as Winnicott does, extends one's thinking, especially if this is located in an intermediary area between two parts of two bodies – mouth and breast – which will create some third object in between them, not just in the actual space that separates them, but in the potential space of their reunion after their separation. This notion of a 'third' object has its application in the psychoanalytic situation. Andre Green (1975) proposes that one understands the exchanges between patient and analyst, or, in other terms, between transference and countertransference processes, as creating an 'analytic third', a specific outcome of analysis.

For Winnicott (1971), in the creation of the 'transitional object', the use that the subject makes of the object is more important than the object used. In other words, in every instance Winnicott holds process as in use over identity as in object. Winnicott alludes to the paradox involved in that use, a paradox, as he said, that has to be accepted, tolerated and respected without forced attempts to solve it. That paradox includes a tolerance of the negative, as is mentioned in his section on symbolism. For Winnicott, its not being the breast (or the mother), although real is as important as the fact that it is an emotional early representation of the breast.

From this conception of normal development (where negative and absence are qualities inherent in psychic functioning, for instance, not-me possession, the paradox of not being and being the breast, as well, and at the same time being a substitute for it, not being an internal object or an external one, but a 'possession', etc.), Winnicott's (1971) work focuses progressively on pathological issues. When things internal to the infant are good-enough, that is to say, not too threatening, the process-related object can prosper, and vice versa; or else, a deadness of the internal object intervenes as a persecutory absence. The internal and external worlds of the infant are mutually dependent in the emotional meaning of the transitional object. It is only the presence or the absence of an object that looks like a transitional one which is meaningful, but the presence or absence are the signs that indicate its quality. It is here that lies such prime importance of absence in psychopathology of the transitional area. For Winnicott, if the absence of the mother extends beyond a tolerable limit, the transitional object (in the emotive power of absence) becomes what Winnicott says is decathected, which means that the memory of the internal representation fades. This fading of the internal representations is what Green relates to the inner representation of the negative, a representation of the absence of representation, which expresses itself in terms of negative hallucination, or in the field of affects, in terms of a void, emptiness, or to a lesser degree futility, meaninglessness. In other words, the absence becomes a bad presence. Absence of memory, absence in the mind, absence of contact, absence of feeling alive – all those absences can be condensed in the idea of a gap. But that gap, instead of referring to a simple void or to something which is missing, becomes the substratum for what is real. Winnicott (1971) says that the only real thing is the gap, that is to say, the only real thing is what is missing, whether by death or amnesia or absence. When the patient experiences an important amnesia during the session, Winnicott writes that the lost object can lose its reality and that the resulting absence can become the only thing that is real. This blotting out (Winnicott), or negative hallucination (Green), or Freud's repression is different from the merely forgotten.

Winnicott describes a patient who is no longer using a rug (even though it is there), or the therapy, for that matter. Winnicott understands this as an absolute necessity, for reality is more important than comfort. The patient also shows that using the rug would be a sign of forgiveness or that reparation has occurred. If so, the reality of the revenge would fade. In the end, the patient's attitude culminates in the idea that a former analyst (of whom she complained so much) will always be more important to her than the present one. The patient is able to recognize that Winnicott does her more good but has to confess that she likes the former therapist better. The patient said that the absence of him is more real than Winnicott's presence. The patient went on to say that it seems he wanted something that never goes away. This is obvious, but what is missing here is that the bad object is the one that never goes away. And the bad thing whether present or absent, is negative anyway in two ways: as bad and as non-existent. The bad thing has to be there, and if it is not, it is this absence equated with void and emptiness that becomes real, more real than the existing objects that are around. The real thing is the absent thing.

In discussing these ideas about absence with a colleague, he ironically recites a short poem which captures what I am trying to say:

> Yesterday upon the stair
> I met a man who wasn't there.
> He wasn't there again today
> I wish the hell he'll go away.

Winnicott's ideas come very close to Green's when he considers the pathological issues. They both agree, for instance, that as a consequence of unbearable separation, that which is usually described in terms of aggression, anger, destruction, etc., can manifest itself in a very different way. In Winnicott's words what happens is a fading of the internal representation, and in Green's, a destructive negative hallucination of the object. They both think that the mechanism operational here is decathesis. When Winnicott (1971) speaks of the negative side of relationships, he means the gradual default that has to be taken in by the child when parents are not available. The lack of availability of the parents gives rise to two different experiences. One is the feeling of the badness of the object with all the aggression included in crying, screaming, feeling in a state of agitation and turmoil; here the negative is identified with the bad. Otherwise, this unavailability is related to non-presence of the object – what Bion calls the 'no-thing' as different from 'nothing'.

Green does not use the word absence, because in the word absence there is hope of a return of the presence. It is also not a loss because this would mean that the loss could be named. The reference to the negative in this second instance is to the non-existent, the void, the emptiness, in other words, the blankness.

These two aspects should be differentiated. Winnicott's contribution is to show how this negative, the non-existence, will become, at some point the only thing that is real. What happens afterwards is that even if the object reappears, the realness of the object is still related to its non-existence. The return of the presence of the object is not enough to heal the disastrous effects of its too long absence – X, Y and Z have taken place. Non-existence has taken possession of the mind, erasing the representations of the object that preceded its absence. This is an irreversible step, at least until treatment.

For André Green, when one thinks of the early mother–child relationship in Winnicottian terms, one realizes the importance of holding. When the separation occurs, the baby is left alone, the mother's representation may be suspended, and replaced by many substitutes. What is of the greatest importance is the introjected construction of a framing structure analogous to the mother's arms in the holding. The framing structure can tolerate the absence of representation because it holds the psychic space, like Jung's and Bion's container, and Plato's receptacle. As long as the framing structure 'holds' the mind, the negative hallucination can be replaced by hallucinatory wish fulfilment or fantasy. But when the baby is confronted with the death experience, the frame becomes unable to create substitute representations – it holds only the void; this means the non-existence of the object or of any substitute object. The negative hallucination of the object cannot be overcome; the negative does not lead to an alternative positive situation. Even the badness of the object and fantasized destructiveness will not do. It is the mind, that is, mental activity giving birth to representations, which is under the threat of being destroyed, in the frame. At other times, it is the framing structure itself that is damaged: here one has disintegration.

What is described here is constant in these cases, many of them presenting negative therapeutic reaction. In fact, in these cases, neither the analyst nor the patient exist periodically in the session. Defences are mobilized each time the material gets closer to anything that is significant. The patient's mind stops registering the interpretations of the analyst. The interpretations are blotted out, the patient says his mind is blank, no associations are provided. The analytic process is paralyzed for some time. One is struck by the fact that these patients seem so vulnerable, so fragile, and though they have extreme rigidity and stubbornness, are animated by hidden feelings of revenge, which they express in an impossibility to change, or to invest in new fields of experience.

The subject is creating the object, in the sense of finding externality itself. This experience depends on the object's capacity to survive – not to retaliate. This destructive activity is the patient's attempt to place the analyst outside the area of omnipotent control, that is, out in the world. Without the experience of maximum destructiveness the patient never places the analyst outside, using the analyst as a projection of a part of the Self the patient will never change. The possible changes depend on the analyst's survival of the attacks, which involves and includes the idea of the absence of a quality of change – change of attitude, quality, etc. – to retaliation.

The analyst feels like interpreting, but it is better if he refrains – absence of interpretation till the heat has passed, otherwise the patient will experience it as the therapist's retaliation.

It is interesting to note that, in Plato's (1965) *Timaeus*, his intuition about the necessary absence is not obvious, that is, it is almost absent, even though the opening of *Timaeus* starts with the missing fourth. Similarly, the importance of the negative and of absence is not obvious in Winnicott's work. If, in *Timaeus*, the creation of the world and of human beings in it seems to take precedence, with Winnicott's the concept of the transitional object and transitional phenomena does. Even though one of the main aspects of these concepts is that they denote 'absence', it is the first 'not-me' possession. This implies the idea of something that is not present – absent. It is both in the absence, and in the absence of explanation in both Plato and Winnicott that one finds the essence of what they are describing. And, in that sense, its very omission – its absence – poignantly emphasizes and illustrates its method and its content.

Absence in Other Pathological States of Mind

I bring this chapter to a close by briefly describing claustrophobia and agoraphobia. Clinical material is drawn in to illustrate absence – and future – as lived and felt experience.

Pathological states of mind such as claustrophobia and agoraphobia are also related to absence. The space, either inside the object as in claustrophobia or outside the object as in agoraphobia is intolerable because these spaces represent emotions indistinguishable from the place where nothing was. That is, in those patients who cannot tolerate the absence of the object, there is a present non-existent object which renders the space frightening. Panic is being trapped in this space with no means of escape, that is, there can be no thought by which escape could be effected.

Pain and suffering cannot be absent from the personality. This is the normal state of affairs that all individuals need to negotiate for benign psychological–emotional development and living. Perhaps one can even say that psychoanalytic discourse as a whole, inasmuch as Plato's dialogues – especially *Timaeus* – depends more or less on absence. For example, most of what is said by the patient in the session is interpreted in connection with the transference, as if concerning someone else, in a relationship which refers to another space and to another time.

A female patient arrived for her first session. Almost immediately she told me that she had already had ten years of therapy twice a week, in which her therapist had not found anything, by which she meant sexual abuse, or any major trauma. She then said: "I have been depressed all my life, but I do not think you are going to find anything either. I had a loving childhood".

We remained silent for a few minutes. I began to feel strange and confused, as if disembodied, while observing the patient fixedly staring at the ceiling, somewhat absent-mindedly. Another while elapsed when I said: "I think our therapy is going to be important not for what we find, but for what is missing".

The patient returned, metaphorically speaking, and appeared interested. She said mockingly: "Oh yes, like the Emperor's new clothes – nobody can see them, and yet, the poor fool is convinced of being dressed up".

Following up from this wonderful opening session, our therapy has been based on absence and sickness – physical and emotional. During the first few years, whenever we touched on something emotionally challenging, the patient would stare at the ceiling, the wall, the floor, or else, she would pull the threads of her woolly jumpers meticulously, in a methodical ritual. Long hours of transfixation, and not knowing what was going on, or what to say, have been the main feature of our work. I would let it be for a shorter or longer period of time ... depending, and constantly gauging my own feelings and the situation, at times, unable to feel anything myself and cut off from my own thinking capacity. Then, I would ask her where she was. More often than not, she would reply that she did not know, but certainly not in the room.

I often pondered about the tragedy of her having been emotionally abandoned and, as a consequence, abandoning herself. The one suffering the absence, now the absented.

Over time, she came to describe a simple pattern of black and white squares that she was creating in her mind and projecting towards the external surfaces. Painstakingly and, in my opinion, enabled by the endurance of not-knowing, we have gained some insight into her experience, and have given some meaning to her idiosyncratic way of dealing with an emotionally absent mother, therapist and Self. Over the years, my patient has become more engaged with herself and with me, and her abstraction into geometrical figures has disappeared. However, whenever we come close to her suffering absence, and more prominently, to her terrifying fear of the potential new, if no longer absenting herself, she complains of developing there and then a throbbing headache, which she blames me for. If only I could let her be in her absent world. Let me clarify that when I speak of the patient's terror of the 'potential new', I do not mean just completely novel experiences, but the novelty of enduring and being aware of her own pain, without running away from it. That is, suffering her pain in a way that can be transformed into something else, as opposed to just feeling pain in a kind of a vacuum which does not evolve.

Therapy continues to be challenging for both of us. But we both have also come to enjoy it, and to be playful together. She is grateful that I do not abandon her in her deadening state of being, from which she now has a desire to liberate herself.

I cannot emphasize enough the value in this therapy, and in psycho-analytic work in general, of 'Negative Capability', as Keats calls it. This is the theme of the following chapter.

References

Bion, W. R. (1962). *Second Thoughts*. London: Maresfield Library/Karnac, 1967.

Freud, S. (1917). Mourning and melancholia. *Standard Edition*, vol. 6.

Green, A. (1975). *The analyst symbolization and absence in the analytic setting. Reprinted in On Private Madness*. London: Hogarth, 1986.

Green, A. (1983). The dead mother. *On Private Madness*. Maddison, CT: International Universities Press. 1986.

Green, A. (1986a). *On Private Madness*. London: Hogarth, 1986.

Green, A. (1986b). The death drive, negative narcissism, and the disobjectalizing function. *The Work of the Negative*. Translated by A. Weller. London: Free Association Books.

Plato. (1965). *Timaeus and Critias*. Translated by D. Lee. London: Penguin.

Shakespeare, W. (1595/1596). *A Midsummer Night's Dream*. Oxford: Clarendon Press.

Steiner, J. (1993). *Psychic Retreats*. London: Routledge.

Whitehead, A. N. (1929). *Process and Reality*. Corrected ed., D. R. Griffin and D. W. Sherburne, Eds. New York: The Free Press, 1985.

Winnicott, D. W. (1963). Dependence in infant care, in child care, and in the psychoanalytic setting. *The Maturational Process and the Facilitating Environment*. London: Karnac.

Winnicott, D. W. (1971). *Playing and Reality*. London: Pelican Books.

Chapter 5

Negative Capability

Introduction

Negative capability is considered as an aspect of absence. It involves the act of emptying oneself of knowledge, ignoring coherence and enduring a state of not-knowing in which confusion, doubt and conflict reign, sometimes unaware. This is conducive to bringing the individual closer to his psychic reality since it facilitates access to intuition, excites curiosity and evokes phantasies. Although the activation of negative capability appears to be a conscious act it is not entirely so since it can depend on the capacity of the unconscious. Whitehead's theory of prehension brings further insight into negative capability as intrinsic to man's nature. Whitehead's theory of prehension states that the essence of experience is that it is a prehending (feeling) thing. The process of prehension includes negative prehension with its own selective form, however trivial or faint. For Whitehead, it is from a background of unconscious activity of prehension that the experiential process of becoming evolves.

Keats's Definition of Negative Capability

This chapter begins with Keats's definition of negative capability.

John Keats (1952[1817]) coined the term 'Negative Capability' in a letter he wrote to his brother. He said:

> I had not a dispute but a disquisition with Dike on obvious subjects; several things dove-tailed in my mind, and at once it struck me what a quality went to form a Man of Achievement, especially in Literature, and which Shakespeare possessed so enormously – I mean

DOI: 10.4324/9781003261841-6

Negative Capability, that is, when a man is capable of being in uncertainties, mysteries, doubts, without irritable reaching after facts and reason.

Aspects of Negative Capability

Socrates's 'Not-knowing'

Psychoanalytic work too demands that in order to be open to a wider consciousness, therapists give importance to the state of 'not-knowing'. In order to know, the therapist must enable and allow for an internal state of not-knowing in both participants of the dialogue. That is, the therapist knows something about the potential of empty-space, as it were, the emergent container of absence.

One may wonder if this is precisely what Oedipus could not tolerate and thus, in not wanting to be ignorant, he had to become all-knowing, at his peril.

For Socrates and Plato the aim of life is to know yourself. Both gave importance to the inscription at the Temple of Delphi: 'to know Yourself' (The Laws XI). Yet, Socrates's highest achievement was to 'reach ignorance' – he knew that he did not know: "I only know that I know nothing". He knew that the truth one knows is not of what 'is', but of what is happening. As recited from Socrates in Plato's *Theaetetus* (1997, pp. 169–170, para. e),

> What is really true, is this: the things of which we naturally say that they 'are', are in process of coming to be, as the result of movement and change and blending with one another. We are wrong when we say they 'are', since nothing ever is, but everything is coming to be.

In Plato's *Timaeus*, absence, the state of not-knowing is the beginning. In Plato's *Apology*, Socrates tells us that he thought to himself:

> I am a wiser man than this man; it is likely that neither of us knows anything worthwhile, but he thinks he knows something when he does not, whereas when I do not know, neither do I think

I know, so I am likely to be wiser than he to this small extent, that I do not think I know what I do not know.

Similarly, in Plato's *Cratylus*, Socrates tells Hermogenes: "the first and finest line of investigation, which as intelligent people must acknowledge, is this, that we admit that we know nothing". And then, in Plato's *Letter VII*, the Athenian says to Clinias:

> we mustn't assume we will be able to look upon reason and get to know it adequately: let's not produce darkness at noon, so to speak, by looking at the sun directly. We can save our sight by looking at an image of the object we are asking about.

This is a crucial point, because so often therapist and patient alike, in their quest to know, get blinded by light. In other words, knowledge may be the psychoanalytic aim, but also its dead-end, for it blinds as much as it reveals. One wants to know – the therapeutic aim is to enable a movement of mind in which unconscious thinking has a place, so that it can be integrated in conscious life, and, thereby, transcend it. But one needs to be able to recognize that one cannot know the-thing-in-itself, the ultimate truth, the unknowable, and perhaps all that one can look at is an image in the form of thoughts, ideas, dreams, feelings, actions, utterances, visual images, etc. To experience symbolizing is to be opened to the richness of mind and life and to its evolving meaning. As Socrates (*Theaetetus*, Plato, 1997, p. 169, para. d) says: "There is nothing which in itself is just one thing".

Jung's Active Imagination

In the *Liber Novus* (*Red Book*, 2009), Jung states the importance of active imagination, which he distinguished from dreams and other forms of spontaneous symbolization. He speaks of these two streams as being generally independent. This notion can be linked to Bion's two methods of thinking: conscious thinking, and thought that comes to the person; a thinker engaging in the process of thinking, and thoughts without a thinker.

For Jung, the technique for inducing spontaneous fantasies – active imagination – he expresses as follows: the training consists first of all in systematic exercises for eliminating critical attention (negative capability); thus producing a vacuum in consciousness – emptying, as opposed to filling. (Note that this is also Freud's recommendation for the psycho-analytic process: to let go of critical judgement in the mind of both the therapist and the patient, so that the former can do his job in an open-minded spirit, and the latter can free-associate without prejudice).

One commences by concentrating on the particular mood, that is, it is the feeling, or the feeling–tone, as vague or as accentuated as it might be, to start with – that is the key to understanding. The feeling–tone as container, both focused enough and flexible enough for exploration and discovery – and attempting to become as conscious as possible of all fantasies and associations that come up in connection with it. The aim was to allow the phantasy free play, without departing from the initial affect, in a free associative process. This leads to a concrete or symbolic expression of the mood, which had the result of bringing the affect nearer to consciousness, hence making it more understandable. Doing this could have a vitalizing effect. Individuals could draw, paint, or sculpt, depending on their propensities. Visual types could concentrate on the expectation that an inner image could be produced. As a rule, such a fantasy–image will actually appear – perhaps hypnagogically – and should be carefully noted down in writing. Auto-verbal types usually hear inner words, perhaps mere fragments or apparently meaningless sentences to begin with. Others, at such times, simply hear their 'other' voice. Still rarer, but equally valuable, is automatic writing.

Once these fantasies had been produced and embodied, two approaches were possible; creative formulation and understanding. Each needs the other, and both were necessary to produce the transcendent function, which arose out of the union of conscious and unconscious contents.

For some people, Jung noted, it was simple to know the 'other' voice in writing, and to answer it from the standpoint of the 'I', as if a dialogue were taking place between two human beings. This dialogue led to the creation of the transcendent function, which resulted in a widening consciousness. This depiction of inner dialogues and the means of evoking fantasies in a waking state represents Jung's own undertaking in the *Black Books*. The interplay of creative formulation and understanding corresponds to Jung's work in *Liber Novus* (2009).

Throughout his work, Jung is emphasizing both the need for negative capability, in order to open the necessary mental space for emergence, and the positive capability in order to work together – both conscious and unconscious and patient and therapist. This is another way of binding the opposites together and creating something new. His scientific endeavour was to see what took place when the individual switches off consciousness. The example of dreams indicated the existence of background activity (this agrees with Freud's view regarding dreams, slips of the tongue, bungled actions, etc.), and he wanted to give this the possibility of emerging. In an entry in his 'Dream Book' on April 17, 1917, Jung noted that since then he had carried out frequent exercises in the emptying of consciousness.

His procedure was clearly intentional – active imagination – while his aim was to allow psychic contents to appear spontaneously. He recalled that beneath the threshold of consciousness, everything was animated – his confrontation with the unconscious.

Reverie itself, one of the main tools at the therapist's disposal, is a dream-like state by its very nature of emptying, allowing for all possibilities to emerge. Of course, this is a notion that the Eastern mind may well be more equipped to deal with than the Western one.

The importance of reaching ignorance, as Socrates, Plato and Jung advocated, lies in reaching wisdom through ignorance, and how learning, growing, awareness and attention, like anything else in psychic life, carries with it something positive and something negative – opening and closure, our blessing and our curse.

For Jung, as for Plato and Socrates, to know yourself is the aim of life, and this means to come to know your other side, without suppressing or repressing, so that one can both enjoy and control the whole range of capacities.

The transcendent function as Jung calls it is the faculty of the psyche by which one is rendered capable of the work of gaining release from the claims of one or the other of the pair of opposites – conscious and unconscious. Similarly, knowing contains not knowing in the pair of opposites. Jung (1928) says that the unconscious is a carrier of memories lost to consciousness, but it is also an intuitive agent of receptivity far exceeding that of the conscious mind. Whitehead (1929), too, speaks of receptivity; reception as opposed to, and included in perception. It is from this reception, or intuiting, which already knows what one does not know consciously, that one pursues knowledge. For Whitehead, in ignoring we create – to get really into a subject takes more energy than 'nothing too much', and man has to ignore much to get on with something. Indeed, what one omits is as important as what one selects, including not only what one knows one is omitting, and what one does not know one is omitting.

Whitehead's Negative Prehension

For Whitehead, as for the psychotherapists, unconscious processes are the emergent container for human experience, including the more basic or the final real things of which the world is made up – an 'actual occasion', an 'actual entity', an act of experience or a 'drop of experience' – and the more 'sophisticated' human consciousness, as well as any mode of experience in between. For Whitehead (1929), the personal identity of a man is a matrix for all transitions of life changed and variously figured by the things that enter it. In other words, "the essence of an actual entity consists solely in the fact that it is a prehending thing" (Ibid., p. 41). For Whitehead (Ibid., p. 53) "consciousness presupposes experience and not experience consciousness … thus an actual entity may, or may not be conscious of some part of its experience". At the same time, "each negative prehension has its own selective form, however trivial and faint. It adds to the emotional complex, though not to the objective data" (Ibid., p. 41). In his idiosyncratic way, Whitehead emphasizes negative capability since it is from a background of unconscious activity of prehension that the experiential process of becoming evolves, and not from conscious realization which is the culmination of this process. Whitehead (1925) says something to the effect that the communion of saints is the great and inspiring assemblage but it has only one possible hall of meeting and that is the present. Whitehead (1933) elaborates this view further, thereby intensifying support for negative capability. He says that all that we can observe consists of conceptual conceptions in the present. Literature presumes the wisdom of the human race, but in this way it enfeebles the emphasis of first hand intuition in considering our direct observation of past, or of future. For him, we should confine ourselves to time spans of the order of magnitude of a second or even of fragments of a second.

For Eigen (2012), too, growth happens when one is not looking. And Bion (1962) called faith the psychoanalytic attitude – psychoanalytic faith which includes openness to what is unknown in a session, and unknown realities that exert transforming impacts.

Freud's Notion of Negation

In *On Negation* (1925), Freud too was talking of negative capability when he wrote that ordinary reality may be an avoidance, like disavowal, that is, it may be used defensively, but negation is also important in freeing thinking from repression. It is certainly essential for psychoanalytic work. The psychoanalytic stance requires a resistance to the pull of ordinary reality or the familiar, so as to stay in the realm of psychic reality. In listening to what patients are presenting, the therapist is listening to what they are communicating about their inner world. By listening in this way, one is setting aside the first meaning of the material that presents itself, that is, it is a negating of ordinary reality in order to go beyond it, towards meaning. It is a move from the literal, to the thing-in-itself, or from the beta-elements towards its meaning and depth, towards alpha-function, towards representing one's experiences to oneself. If psychic reality is constituted by representation, and representation depends on an act of negation, that makes negation an essential element in the constitution of psychic reality. The analytic setting itself is a presentation of the mind, of internal mental structure, for it not only gives access to it, but embodies it. The analytic setting is in the nature of emergent container, a place of reflection and withdrawal of attention from the outside world. Any experiencing of oneself as subject has to be achieved against an essential background of loss and absence – negative capability.

Bion's Views on 'Without Memory or Desire'

Throughout his writings, Bion advocates the negative capability of the therapist, that is, to carry out the work 'without memory or desire', so that the present can emerge – so that the present is not obscured, or filled with memories and desires.

Man hates to think that he is ignorant. To endure the absence of memory and desire is excruciating for both participants in the analytic dialogue. There seems to be an investment in knowing the answer, or the individual is pressured from within and from without to produce one, and foreclose the discussion. The therapist, the doctor, is the one supposed to know, so he does not want to be, or even appear to be, ignorant, and, by doing so, like Oedipus, he runs the risk of becoming all-knowing. It is not easy; patients are suffering, fearful, confused, and yet a further absence is requested of them – to reach ignorance with the therapist.

Two Values of Negative Capability

Negative Capability as Defensive Purposes

One may wonder if when Keats was speaking of 'Negative Capability', he was not describing two very different capacities; one which closes the container, and the other which opens it. That is to say, the negative capability refers to both the capacity to close off what one does not want to hear, as in unconscious defence mechanisms such as repression, regression, denial, hallucination, disavowal, etc. And, equally, it refers to enduring uncertainty, chaos, confusion, doubts and not-knowing, so that something new can emerge.

Negative capability has a dual meaning both as the source of growth and emergence, as the source of transcendent function, and as defensive purposes – psychological defence mechanisms which happen to be survival mechanisms of the psyche. Escapism, in one form or another is, after all, basic to human nature as a form of self-cure, and as an attempt to protect one's Self and/or ego from unbearable anxieties. The infant, unwilling to be aware of its helplessness, already idealizes or ignores. He already resorts to omnipotence as an antidote for help-lessness. He already brings the body to redress the unpleasantness of the mind and vice versa.

Freud connected negative therapeutic reaction, that is, the patient's attempt to sabotage any possible benefit thus far obtained through psychoanalytic treatment, or even the ending of the treatment alto-gether, to the Death Instinct, and formed an hypothesis of primary narcissism (1937). This notion is similar to Green's (1983) 'narcissism of death', by which the narcissistically wounded infant identifies with a dead mother object.

Freud (1924) suggests that the need for punishment is a better term for what he originally described as an urge to minimize an unconscious sense of guilt, and linked concealed masochistic tendencies to the occurrence of the negative therapeutic reaction. Here, as in "Beyond the Pleasure Principle" (1920) and elsewhere, Freud is putting forward the notion that the compulsion to repeat is fundamental, basic to the human mind, even more so than to obtain pleasure or to avoid pain.

In a similar vein to Freud and Green, Sandler et al. (1973), describe the negative therapeutic reaction as the patient's regression into the image of the depressed loved and hated mother.

Negative Capability as a Source of Growth and Emergence

Taking now the other meaning of negative capability, while preserving Freud's and Klein's contributions, Bion adds freshness by emphatically emphasizing the value of negative capability, by insisting that one approaches the task of psychoanalysis 'without memory or desire'. This creates uncertainty, which, in turn, increases creative capacity, and the development of intuition, helping the therapist into a state of reverie, or a state of discovery. Bion's language, like Plato's and Jung's, contains what appears as doubts, half-doubts, mysteries and uncertainties. The basic assumption of psychoanalysis is that if the mind can create fallacious solutions, the mind can correct them, as well.

Bion's reverie, Freud's free-floating attention and Jung's *abaissement* involve negative capability of detaching oneself from an almost addictive attachment to memory and thinking, and thereby letting the experience speak for itself. They believe that insight comes suddenly and unexpectedly, if only one has the patience to wait; it does not come when one is in 'the thinking mood', but in a flash, on a trivial occasion, in a mental relaxation. In this state of reverie, an image of some sort, or a memory, or a feeling may float in one's mind, as it were, which, as a symbol of psychic reality, may be extremely important. But for this to happen, one needs to let go on the one hand, and, on the other, to be in inner emotional readiness that can open out into a new and unexpected field of enquiry. Bion follows the Platonic concept of 'thoughts without a thinker', that is, thoughts that will only reach the individual when he is ready to receive them. Consequently, Bion, like Jung, Whitehead and Plato, encourages the therapist to let go of psychological comfort, venture forth into the unknown, and risk the terror. Earlier on, Freud too had given importance to advising patients to say whatever came into their minds – free-association – without passing judgement and without sanitizing it. Freud had emphasized the importance of making the unconscious conscious, so that the person is not fully ruled by it. For that, the capacity to remember was pivotal for, in remembering, the repression could be lifted. For Bion (1977, p. 3), however, the capacity to remember needs to be allied to a capacity for forgetting – negative capability – so that the fact that any session is a new session, and therefore an unknown situation that must be psychologically investigated, is not obscured by an already over-plentiful fund of preconceptions and misconceptions.

In *Cogitations* (posthumously published and written between 1958 and 1979), Bion states that the inability to tolerate empty space limits the amount of space available. In other words, if all psychic space (whatever that might actually mean) is saturated, filled-in or filled-up, there is no room for the new. This is also the view of Milner (1957) in her notion of 'pregnant emptiness'. That is, a no-mind state of being, or a negative capability which allows the new to enter. Mental space is understood as a thing-in-itself that is unknowable, but that can be represented in thoughts. But, the notion of approaching psychoanalytic sessions 'without memory or desire', that is, this form of negative capability, also has its problems. To begin with, it is part of man's humanity to desire, to remember, to wish, to hope. Secondly, negative capability is the capacity of the mind which depends on the capacity of the unconscious, while 'no memory and desire' can only apply to a conscious attitude. As much or as little as it is possible or desirable to be with no memory or desire, any encounter with oneself/other is based on preconceptions and therefore in memories, or some kind of memory and influence, whether conscious or unconscious, whether personal or archetypal. What is more, any encounter with Self/other is already propelling towards future possibilities and desires. In short, man's unconscious will continue to operate in its compensatory and other intrinsic ways regardless of his conscious attitudes. Jung wrote in his letters that the unconscious is a piece of nature our mind cannot comprehend. That is to say, man does not know his unconscious, but only its manifestations, and even those, he still needs to interpret.

For Freud (1926), there is more continuity in emotional life than is evident in the act of birth. This applies both literally to the act of being born and a continuity with a life in the womb, and to the psychological birth which brings with it an immeasurable wealth of archetypal potential.

Similarly, in "Transformations" (1965), Bion makes it clear that no one can ever know what happens in the analytic session, the thing-in-itself, 'O'; one can only speak of what the therapist or the patient feels happens: his emotional experience. One knows what the participants say happens, or the emotional state engendered by the verbalizations of therapist and patient in the listener. Something certainly happens, but it is the therapist's task to discern whether there is an emotional response or merely something which represents it – the interpretations draw attention to an existing emotional state, but it produces the emotional state of awareness of an emotional state. In fact, the decision depends on whether one thinks the analyst or patient works in words or in emotions.

Bion's theory of transformation, enabled by negative capability and state of reverie is intended to illuminate a chain of phenomena in which the understanding of one link, or aspect of it, helps in the understanding of others. This may sound like a linear way of thinking, but it is more than that, for the emphasis of this enquiry is on the nature of the transformation in a psychoanalytic session.

For Bion, the correct analysis (if such a thing exists) demands that the analyst's interpretation should formulate what the patient's behaviour reveals; conversely, that the analyst's judgement should be embodied in an interpretation and not in an emotional discharge. To this one may add provisionally that this contribution may be regarded as embodied in the change of the patient's emotional state. The emphasis is on the growth of the patient's thought, as well as wealth and intensity of experience.

Bion (1977), turns our attention to our difficulties in assessing which of our capacities are of any value, particularly in knowing what is going on. In the light of process it is hard to know the person today, tomorrow or in the future. This flies in the face of the then current object relations theory for which knowing the past is the main source of understanding. Negative capability, this not-knowing is, at its best, allied to one's capacity to make room for a pre-conception that will illuminate a problem and excite curiosity.

Bion questions how we learn anything, if our judgement is based on experience, that is, in what is already known. He says that, as a rule, it is never based on what is new, what is still unknown, and that under certain conditions might considerably enrich the directed process. Bion answers the question by advocating negative capability; by approaching the session with no memory or desire, for the capacity to forget and the ability to eschew desire and understanding are essential to maintain one's power of observation. One way of expressing this view is that the person learns from experience, and learning from experience is a process in which negative capability plays an important role.

Whitehead (1938, p. 6) agrees. He states that "in order to acquire learning, we must shake ourselves free of it". And, in 1929 he says that, in his view, spontaneity arises from "empty space" – "Life itself is a characteristic of empty space" (p. 105). This is how crucial negative capability is for man's own existence, or, better, for his quality of existence – for that thing called life.

It is better to know – to know yourself – but in order to get to know, one must allow for not-knowing. That is, one needs to empty oneself of knowledge, in order for it to emerge afresh. For it is this negative capability which will stimulate one's curiosity about the vast, the infinite, domain of his ignorance. In *Timaeus*, negative capability, or the not-knowing attitude is the original expression of continual awareness that one does not know – Socrates does not know where the fourth is. The inevitable may be known, but the possible is not. One needs to ignore coherence – negative capability – so that one is confronted by incoherence, and the experience of incomprehension presented to him. To tolerate this emotional experience, which may involve doubt and persecution – persecutory feelings – the painful nature of the dilemma is essential. At times, the material, the situation and/or the experience may appear familiar, perhaps even repetitive and monotonous to both participants. That is, it may seem to relate to what is already known. But, the obvious, or what seems already known, must also, or particularly, be experienced anew every time, for each time it will be different – what seems like a repetitive circle or cycle may actually be a spiral. The endurance, suffering and tolerance of frustration between the oscillation between patience and security, pain and pleasure, paranoid–schizoid and depressive position must prevail for the development of meaning.

Plato's *Letter VIII* reads: "what seems to be the end of a difficulty always involves the beginning of a new one". Learning is always in process, like life itself; it is always becoming. Learning takes time to develop, it has to be experienced, and the more one learns, as Socrates knew, the more one should find how ignorant one is. There is an inexhaustible fund of ignorance to draw upon. This is man's wisdom, his negative capability. But, of course, a state of mind between being ignorant and intellectually aware is very difficult to achieve, and it calls for courage.

In the *Laws VII*, the Athenian states that our goal should be "to live the life that our own nature demands". This is at the heart of Jung's emergence of the Self, and Winnicott's True Self. But to achieve this, or to fully understand what it means, is a different matter. As mentioned earlier, it is as if one can never know the thing-in-itself, but only secondary and primary qualities, whilst, on the other hand, the only thing one can know is the thing-in-itself. As Whitehead (1929, p. 145) puts it: "the percipient occasion is its own standard of actuality". This could be understood to mean that the experience, the emotion, the feeling has its own lines of meaning and interpretation – it is self-evident, it simply is.

In his poem ("Vala: Night the Second)", William Blake (1797) speaks of what experience entails: desolate wisdom.

> What is the price of experience? Do men buy it
> for a song?
> Or wisdom for a dance in the street? No, it is
> bought with the price
> of all that a man hath, his house, his wife, his
> children,
> wisdom is sold in the desolate market where none
> come to buy,
> and in the wither'd field where the farmer plows
> for bread in vain.

And Yeats (1933) in his poem "Crazy Jane" reminds us that:

> Love has pitched its mansion
> in the place of excrement
> and nothing can be sole or
> whole that has not been rent.

For Wittgenstein (2000), if in life we are surrounded by death, so too in the health of our understanding by madness.

In both Jung's archetypes and Bion's pre-conceptions, the potential lies in emptiness, in absence, in what they are not – neither are unconscious representations or perceptions. They are potentials, emergent containers, symbols, images which are not actually present to the ego, and yet they are very real. What can be repressed and forgotten belongs to the personal, and what cannot, belongs to the archetypal.

Bion (1979) asks why so much more emphasis and validity is placed on the waking state, as opposed to the dreaming state.

Freud's interpretation of dreams, Jung's archetypal and alchemical notions, Whitehead's speculative philosophy, Bion's ideas about the need to forget, so that one can develop dream–thoughts, and his whole mythological theory of alpha and beta functions and elements, inasmuch as Plato's *Timaeus*, express a balanced attitude between waking and dreaming, and, above all, they express the value of negative capability.

Another way in which negative capability is of great value in psychoanalytic work manifests in the capacity to listen to silence – to what silence is saying, for silence talks, it communicates through the eloquent language of silence. If one is constantly talking, it is impossible to hear the silence. This is true of psychoanalytic sessions, and of life in general. It only takes a one-minute silence for painful emotions to be stirred, personally and collectively.

Winnicott's Contribution to Negative Capability

Winnicott was also well aware of the importance of negative capability in psychoanalytic work. Winnicott (1963) speaks of the notion of us needing to fail our patients. For him, the therapist failure is his success. What Winnicott means by this is that the therapist fails the patient in familiar ways, giving rise to familiar regressive patterns. This time, however, the containing function of the therapist introduces the differential factor. From this receptacle, a strengthened ego and a new dependency can emerge in which the patient can bring the bad external factor into his omnipotent control and under the mechanisms of projection and projective identification. This is far from being a single theory of cure by corrective experience but, rather, it refers to process, containment and renewal.

Furthermore, Winnicott defines the creation of the transitional object as a 'not-me' possession. The object is here defined as a negative of me, which has implications with regard to omnipotence. For Winnicott (1971) in the creation of the 'transitional object', the use that the subject makes of the object is more important than the object used. In other words, in every instance Winnicott holds process as in use over identity as in object. Winnicott here alludes to the paradox involved in that use, a paradox, as he said, that has to be accepted, tolerated and respected, without forced attempts to solve it. That paradox involves a tolerance of the negative. For Winnicott (1971), it is not being the breast (or the mother) that is important as the fact that it is an emotional early representation of the breast.

Green (1983), influenced by Winnicott, especially *Playing and Reality*, and his concept of 'transitional object and transitional phenomena' (1951), introduced *The Work of the Negative* (*Le Travail du Negatif*, 1986). Green points out that the clinical material Winnicott presented entitled 'String' shows how the sense of loss itself can become a way of integrating one's Self experience (1971).

One may add that it can only be the sense of loss that can either help one to integrate his experiences, or else, to lose himself – the individual embodies absence and absence embodies the individual. To constitute absence may be among the person's most vital tasks. For Plato, it is out of absence, out of what is not, out of the missing fourth, out of sickness that the whole world and human beings emerge. The whole island of Atlantis disappeared, but it left behind a residue for the potential new. The negative (capability) is implicit in everything the therapist does in the consulting room, and in his psychoanalytic concepts. Starting with Freud, the unconscious implies a reference to the negative, not only because it is not conscious, but, also, because in Freud's descriptions, when he thinks of the relationship between two conscious representations, in a free-association context, he has to postulate the existence of an unconscious thought or representation between them. Here the negative is associated with the idea of a latent something operating behind the scenes, invisible though active. In identification, too, the relationship has no visible contact except the one established in the mind. Processes take place in the negative. Absence is directly related to the negative as that which is not present – not positively perceived through the senses. In Freud's theory of drives, there is an implication of something in excess of the psychic apparatus which has to be reduced or repressed or, as Green calls it 'negativated'. The journey of Freud's work could be described as starting from neurosis as the negative of perversion, towards the negative therapeutic reaction. For Freud, it is out of hallucination of absence that thought/thinking will eventually emerge. It is through mourning that a healthy ego will be born. Psychotherapy itself is a process of mourning.

From an object–relations point of view (as opposed to Freudian drive theory), as mentioned earlier, Winnicott defines the transitional object as a 'not-me' possession, that is, the negative of me. Winnicott treasured the place not to be communicated, the solitude that allows Self-emergence, and the destructiveness (ruthlessness) that embodies the other as separate and apart from ourselves. For Green, absence is the matrix that enables the forming of a creative structure. For Jung, it is through the encounter with the unconscious, with the unknown, the *nigredo*, the shadow and hell itself that the Self is born. For Bion, thought, love and transformation exist only in relation to their negatives. The absence – to be without memory or desire – is a call to the potential emergence of the positive. It is one's devoted absence in presence and presence in absence in the form of reverie that carries with it the greatest potential for the psychological development of the analytic couple. This is how vital the negative capability is for psychoanalytic work.

The patient arrived after an Easter break. He lay down on the couch – silent, motionless, lifeless. The room was filled with absence, the absence full of fears: his and mine. The container was broken, and he and I were separated by an ocean of mistrust. Two complete strangers in the room, even though two weeks before we had been intimately connected by a decade of relationship through psychoanalytic work. Now all lost. At some time, I am not sure when, he began to talk in an almost inaudible voice about his loneliness during the break. He had not spoken to a soul. Nobody phoned, nobody cared. He wishes to sleep ... forever. Life is too painful, too pointless.

My anxiety is increasing. I cannot take his reproach, his lamentation, at least not today. I myself feel physically unwell; a cold has taken most of my voice and my energy away. It feels overwhelming. The clock is not moving. Time has imprisoned the two of us in a deadly empty space. I cannot breathe. I want out.

The patient says that the best way he can articulate his experience during the break is thus: it is as if he has spent two weeks in a locked dungeon, deep underground, and with only a tiny bit of light very high up. Now I know what he means. We are in it.

The session drags on; in fear, in sickness. The deadening absence filled the air with deadness when, out of the blue, out of the blues, the blue sky came up. The patient was literally blinded by a ray of sunlight, and by the frightening realization of his own suffering. He covered his eyes with both hands. We talked about this immediate experience of what was happening: as painful to be in the dark as to become conscious; as painful to feel numb as to feel something.

Slowly I am beginning to feel closer to him. I wonder what his life must be like, when only a taste of it feels so crushing. I am moved, I am touched, I feel empathy mixed up with despondency and anger. The session is coming to a close. I tell him something to the effect that it has been important for him to let me know about the impact of my absence, of my abandoning him during the break, and to make me feel it. He confirms this, expands on it, and eventually tells me that "only with me does he feel he has a right to exist". I feel emotional as we say goodbye. We have lost it and regained it many times over, ever since. The work goes on, and it continues to be emotionally challenging, painful, painfully slow and immensely refreshing. Like the Phoenix, we seem to rise from the ashes, only to become pulverized again and again. A thousand deaths fill our empty hours, and as many times we are resuscitated, live and even laugh ... together. The negative capability is our best ally, for what my patient needs at such moments of utter despair is not a clever interpretation, but my being with him, being witness to his suffering, and sharing his sorrows.

In leaving the exploration of negative capability, two interrelated thoughts emerge for further reflection. One is related to the question of whether psychoanalysis itself is an elaboration to fill the gap of one's frightful ignorance, the other refers to the psychoanalyst search for meaning – feeling and relationship – even when dealing with the meaningless.

References

Bion, W. R. (1958–1979). *Cogitations.* London: Karnac, 1992.

Bion, W. R. (1962). *Second Thoughts.* London: Maresfield Library/Karnac. 1967.

Bion, W. R. (1965). Transformations. *Seven Servants.* New York: Jason Aronson, 1977.

Bion, W. R. (1977). *Taming Wild Thoughts.* London: Karnac.

Bion, W. R. (1979). Making the best of a bad job. *Clinical Seminars and Other Works.* London: Karnac, 1994.

Blake, W. (1797). *Vola: Night the Second.* Edwin John Ellis, William Butler Yeats, 1893. London: Bernard Quarich.

Eigen, M. (2012). *Kabbalah and Psychoanalysis.* London: Karnac.

Freud, S. (1920). Beyond the pleasure principle. *Standard Edition*, 18.

Freud, S. (1924). The economic problem of masochism. *Penguin Freud Library*, 11. London: Penguin.

Freud, S. (1925). On negation. *Standard Edition*, 19.

Freud, S. (1926). Inhibitions, symptoms and anxiety. *Standard Edition*, 20.

Freud, S. (1937). Analysis terminable and interminable. *Standard Edition*, 23.

Green, A. (1983). *The Dead Mother.* London: Hogarth.

Green, A. (1986). *The Work of the Negative.* Translated by A. Weller. London: Free Association Books.

Jung, C. G. (1928). Revision of the Eros theory. Psychology of the unconscious. *Collected Works*, vol. 7. Translated by R. F. C. Hull. London: Routledge & Kegan Paul.

Jung, C. G. (1946). *The Psychology of the Transference.* Translated by R. F. C. Hull. London: Routledge, 1983.

Jung, C. G. (2009). *The Red Book: Liber Novus.* Edited by S. Shamdasani. London: Philemon.

Keats, J. (1952[1817]). *Letters.* Edited by M. B. Forman. 4th ed. London: Oxford University Press.

Milner, M. (1957). *On Not Being Able to Paint.* New York: International University Press.

Plato. *Timaeus and Critias.* Translated by D. Lee. London: Penguin, 1965.

Plato. (1997). Apology. *Plato Complete Works.* Edited by J. M. Cooper and D. S. Hutchinson. Indianapolis: Hackett Publishing.

Plato. (1997). Cratylus. *Plato Complete Works*. Edited by J. M. Cooper and D. S. Hutchinson. Indianapolis: Hackett Publishing.
Plato. (1997). Letter VII. *Plato Complete Works*. Edited by J. M. Cooper and D. S. Hutchinson. Indianapolis: Hackett Publishing.
Plato. (1997). Letter VIII. *Plato Complete Works*. Edited by J. M. Cooper and D. S. Hutchinson. Indianapolis: Hackett Publishing.
Plato. (1997). *Plato Complete Works*. Edited by J. M. Cooper and D. S. Hutchinson. Indianapolis: Hackett Publishing.
Plato. (1997). Theaetetus. *Plato Complete Works*. Edited by J. M. Cooper and D. S. Hutchinson. Indianapolis: Hackett Publishing.
Plato. (1997). The Laws VII. *Plato Complete Works*. Edited by J. M. Cooper and D. S. Hutchinson. Indianapolis: Hackett Publishing.
Plato. (1997). The Laws XI. *Plato Complete Works*. Edited by J. M. Cooper and D. S. Hutchinson. Indianapolis: Hackett Publishing.
Sandler, J., Dare, C. and Holder, A. (1973). *The Patient and the Analyst*. London: Allen & Unwin.
Whitehead, A. N. (1925). *Science and the Modern World*. London: Free Association Books, 1985.
Whitehead, A. N. (1929). *Process and Reality*. Corrected ed., D. R. Griffin and D. W. Sherburne, Eds. New York: The Free Press, 1985.
Whitehead, A. N. (1933). *Adventure of Ideas*. New York: The Free Press, 1967.
Whitehead, A. N. (1938). *Modes of Thought*. New York: The Free Press, 1966.
Winnicott, D. W. (1951). Transitional objects and transitional phenomena: A study of the first not-me possession. *Playing and Reality*. London: Pelican Books, 1972.
Winnicott, D. W. (1963). Dependence in infant-care, in childcare, and in the psychoanalytic setting. *The Maturational Process and the Facilitating Environment*. London: Karnac, 1990.
Winnicott, D. W. (1971). *Playing and Reality*. London: Pelican Books.
Wittgenstein, L. (2000). *Wittgenstein and Psychoanalysis*. New York: Totem Books.
Yeats, W. B. (1933). Cracy Jane talks to the bishop. *The Poems of W. B. Yeats*. London: Macmillan, 1950.

Chapter 6

Experience and Whitehead
"Philosophy is a lure for feeling"
(Whitehead, 1929)

Introduction

In this chapter experience is questioned on two levels: the epistemological as encapsulated in metaphysical thought and the experiential
as the living event in therapeutic practice. Experience is both reflected
upon and studied conceptually and it is also presented as a living
moment, felt, shared and embodied within and between the two
people involved – the analytic couple. Conceptualizations of experience and the immediate experience which patient and therapist enter
into are not identical, but they are mutually referential. In other
words, metaphysical and psychological concepts provide interpretative frameworks for experience. The living experience, in turn,
provides the raw material from which metaphysical concepts evolve.
The intention is to bring concepts into experience and experience into
concepts. Following Plato's, Whitehead's and Freud's ideas, experience is examined as process, and as ultimate reality whose basis is
emotion. Based on clinical material, experience is allowed to speak
for itself.

Whitehead in the Consulting Room

In this section I propose that Whitehead in the consulting room could
equally be expressed as the consulting room in Whitehead. What I
mean by this is that his views on feeling as a basic condition of
experience, relational and transitional, provide elucidation to a fundamental psychoanalytic concern: the immediacy of the experience that
patient and therapist are participating in.

DOI: 10.4324/9781003261841-7

Experience, Feeling and Consciousness

For Whitehead (1929, p. 85), "the subjective aim is not primarily intellectual; it is the lure for feeling. This lure for feeling is the germ of mind". By mind, here Whitehead means the complex of mental operations – which do not necessarily involve conscious awareness – involved in the constitution of an actual entity. Whitehead states that "the primary function of theories is as a lure for feeling, thereby providing immediacy of enjoyment and purpose" (Ibid., p. 184) and that "propositions are lures for feeling" (Ibid., p. 208). From this perspective one could say that psychotherapy is a lure for feeling; it is an experience, an emotional experience, an adventure and, by its very own nature, one impossible to describe. This difficulty in description and definition is due to the fact that experience is not only constantly unfolding, but it is also constantly constructed and interpreted. The experience itself is always complete and true, and partial: incomplete and biased. It is complete in that the experience, the feeling or the emotion is its own meaning – it is self-evident, it simply is. It is incomplete in that much of it is precognitive, and also in the sense that man cannot perceive the whole and the infinite and biased, for one selects from something which is already selected.

Plato too emphasized the value of experience. In *Letter VIII*, he states that "experience seems to be the truest test of any matter". And, in *The Laws*, Plato says that "a broader and culturally deeper education and range of experience are needed to produce truly good beings". Similarly for Whitehead, experience is what really matters: it has value. More than value, it is the very essence of the universe – value as the intrinsic reality of an event. In *Process and Reality* (1929, pp. 3–4), Whitehead states that he understood metaphysics not as an attempt to talk about things beyond all possible experience, but, actually, as the endeavour to construct a coherent scheme of ideas in terms of which every element of experience can be interpreted. He adds: "elucidation of immediate experience is the sole justification for any thought" (Ibid., p. 167). Whitehead rejects the view that the most elementary units of the world are 'vacuous actualities' meaning entities that are fully actual and yet wholly devoid of experience, in favour of panexperientialism, according to which all actualities have experience. This means that all things are in process and are active and reactive in that sense. That all things have experience does not mean to say that all things have psyches. Inasmuch as the fact that all individuals have experiences, that does not mean that all individuals have consciousness. What is more, even for those individuals who have consciousness, including human beings, it does not mean to say that they have consciousness of all things, or at all times. Indeed, consciousness is a very high level of experience and, as the psychoanalytic endeavour shows, a difficult thing to attain.

For Whitehead, consciousness arises in a late derivative phase of complex integrations, and primarily illuminates the higher phase in which it arises. Accordingly, consciousness only dimly illuminates the primitive elements of experience. In other words, consciousness primarily illuminates the late comers, which have been constructed by the occasion of experience itself, rather than the earlier arrivals, which are given to the occasion of experience from beyond itself. The earlier arrivals, or the 'primitive elements' in experience are those that enter through (non-sensory) perception. Sensory perception is so prominent in consciousness, not because it is man's fundamental form of perception, but precisely because it is not. Thus, "negative perception" – absence, what is not – "is the triumph of consciousness" (Whitehead, 1929, p. 161). The negative point here is that consciousness therefore does not cast a bright searchlight upon these elements of experience that are truly fundamental, in the sense of arising in the initial phase of experience. In other words, man experiences more than he can analyse, and that he can be aware of, and yet, his own experience (even if not completely known in all its phases, and even if constructed) is his best guiding principle. Man cannot know his own experience fully – the thing-in-itself – and yet, this is the best he has. For Plato, man is aware of what something represents but not of what something 'is'.

For Whitehead (1929, p. 162), "the primitive form of physical experience is emotional – blind emotion – received and felt elsewhere in another occasion and conformally appropriated as a subjective passion". Prehension is his more technical term for 'feeling'. Thus, a physical prehension groups a prior occasion of experience, taking some of its feelings into itself. Prehension is a primitive form of sensory perception which also involves an actual grasping of the prehended object, so that some aspect of that object is involved within the prehending experience. The physical prehension is also an orientation towards the future. Each occasion of experience actualizes itself in such a way as to pass an experiential energy to subsequent occasions. The ripples of a process reach all corners of the universe.

Similarly, for William James (1912), consciousness is the subjective form of feeling – an emergent function, a process. In other words, consciousness is a particular function of experience. In *Science and the Modern World,* Whitehead (1933, pp. 144–145) states what that function is: "consciousness is the function of knowing".

The reason why the individual is not generally conscious of the 'physical world'– or 'nature' – as filled with intrinsic value, is that it is only in non-sensory prehension that he experiences other things as value laden. For example, one directly prehends his prior occasions of experience and 'remembers' them with their joys, sufferings and desires. The individual also directly experiences, if in more blurred fashion, his bodily members, feeling their excitement, their enjoyment, their suffering, their thirst and hunger. If one would generalize this knowledge of what the 'physical world' is like, one would not think of it as devoid of values, but as the throbbing multiplicity of energetic, passionate, appetitive events striving for and realizing values. Man has instead assumed, especially in the modern world, that it is his sensory perception, especially vision, that tells him what the physical world is really like. This assumption, according to Whitehead, has had such fateful consequences because, in sensory perception, the element of value is virtually lost – what was received in prehension is transmuted, and the transmutation involves playing down the subjective, emotional nature of the data, and playing up the objective, purely geometrical aspects.

Psychoanalytic encounters matter, they have value. Frequently, neither the therapist nor the patient can (fully) verbalize what happens in the sessions, but they know that they are moved, stimulated, challenged and intrigued. They both know that feelings and imagery are evoked, and that what takes place is important. The experience(s) with the patient(s) is the most important element in psychoanalytic work, and thus, what needs to be understood. However, to speak of experience as the most fundamental factor in psychoanalytic work does not mean to say that one endorses a rigid empiricist view. On the contrary, experience understood in its Whiteheadian meaning, includes both non-sensory perception and reception; direct observation and direct intuitive observation; and the past, present and future becoming one is an event – in an actual experience.

For Whitehead, as for the psychotherapists, relations are fundamental. In other words, an occasion of experience of an 'actual occasion' is what is most fully actual. It might be brief, but it condenses a causal influence of the past upon the present. Its influence is in-fluency, a real in-flowing which affects the present experience. 'Prehension' is Whitehead's term for this internal appropriation of causal influences from the past. He says: "I use the term 'prehension' for the general way in which the occasion of experience can include as part of its own essence, any other entity" (Ibid., p. 234).

For Whitehead, the essence of experience is that it is a feeling (prehending) thing. In 1929 he states: "the essence of an actual entity is that it consist solely of the fact that it is a prehending thing" (Ibid., p. 41). This idea – that occasions of experience are taken up into later occasions of experience – is at the very heart of Whitehead's cosmology. His philosophy, he says, "is mainly devoted to the task of making clear the notion of being present in another entity" (Ibid., p. 50). Following on from this notion, in Whitehead's account, "the primitive element – experience – is sympathy, that is, feeling the feeling in another and feeling conformally with another" (Ibid., p. 162).

For Whitehead, the datum for the very origination of the experience evokes in it a sympathetic subjective form of response to itself, consisting most fundamentally of emotional and appetitive feelings. What Whitehead is saying is that, basically, man perceives other things which are in the world of actualities in the same way as he is. "Our emotions are directed towards other things, including our bodily organs" (Ibid., p. 158). Far from being incidental, this mention of our bodily organs is central to Whitehead's ideas. The person perceives the world external to his body with his body, so that his most direct perception of what he calls 'the physical world' is not his sensory perception of external things, but his reception of feelings from his body. In perceiving his bodily organs, he perceives them as passing on their experiences – which means that he is at least dimly aware they had their own experiences, out of which his experiences arose. We feel with our bodies and our thoughts are feelings made articulate.

Whitehead also criticizes the way that Western philosophical thought from Descartes onward has excessively privileged 'clear and distinct' conscious perception – what Whitehead calls 'presentational immediacy' – ignoring the way that this perception is always already grounded in our bodies, and in the inheritance from the past in the present – through what Whitehead calls 'causal efficacy'. Even when one does represent, one is also feeling his body, and feeling with his body. It is through visceral feelings – intuition – that one has 'feeling of feeling', that is, memory – which is, in effect an actual entity constituting one's own part-occasions of experience of which one has direct awareness. The person can also have such awareness, albeit much less regularly and clearly, about the analogous occasions of experience constituting the psyches of other human beings (and animals). It is in this primary visceral feeling, in this intuition, reverie, receptacle or container that psychoanalytic work is based.

Whitehead's view (1929, p. 166 and pp. 36–38) is that the whole universe consists of elements disclosed in the analysis of subjects. There is no alternative meaning of "togetherness" other than "experiential togetherness", that is to say, of any meaning not abstracted from the experiential meaning (Ibid., p. 189 and pp. 40–50).

The experiences of subjects always involve the experiences of other subjects, and the new actualities would always be the experiences of other subjects. 'Togetherness in experience' means that every experience is a 'stream' of experience, or an 'occasion' of experience. With the former alternative there is togetherness in the stream, and with the latter alternative there is togetherness in the occasion. In either case, there is unique 'experiential togetherness'. "Concrescence is the production of novel togetherness" (Ibid., p. 21). In psychoanalysis, this 'experiential togetherness', mainly the analytic relationship to oneself and to another, is of the essence. Two individuals, patient and therapist, are experientially together in their solitude.

Subjectivity is embedded in the world. The subject is an irreducible part of the universe, of the way things happen. There is nothing outside the experience; and experience always happens to some subject or other. Whitehead's 'ontological principle' asserts that "there is nothing that floats in the world from nowhere. Everything in the actual world is referable to some actual entity" (Ibid., p. 244). Whitehead, like Kant, privileges human subjectivity in that, for him, a final reality is identified with experience, but, unlike Kant, for Whitehead, the temporal world is not merely experienced, but actively entered into (Ibid., p. 190). However, just because something is not experienced, it does not mean to say that it does not exist. And, although there is nothing outside "experience as a constructive functioning", the experience itself is always partial in both senses of the word: incomplete and biased, as well as complete and true. Something will always be left out. Parts of our experience are pre-cognitive and affective, and prehension involves a particular selection – an objectification and an abstraction (Ibid., p. 60) – of the 'data' that are being prehended. Thus, Whitehead's view reminds us that we directly know, through prehensions of one's own body, that the world is comprised of beings with which we can sympathise, and that sympathy is a natural response. His account is also designed to remove the tendency produced by consciousness to see ourselves as cut off from the world. A central purpose of Whitehead's cosmology is to remind man of what he essentially is, below the superficialities of consciousness and sensory perception, with the hope that "the intellectual insight" will be converted "into an emotional force connecting the sensitive experience (Ibid., p. 15). Whitehead (1938, p. 138), states that "an abstraction is nothing else than the omission of part of the truth".

Whitehead's ideas are relevant for psychoanalytic work because the essence of his work, as that of the therapist, is empathy. Whitehead speaks about everything in the universe becoming one – concrescence – and being increased by one, and the therapist speaks of the feeling of becoming 'at-one' (Bion) with his patient(s) through relationship and understanding. In other words, it feels as if empathy is at the heart of what therapists do, as well as of their theories. The latter manifests in Jung's notion of kinship libido, container, vas, reverie, coniunctio, psychic infection; in Klein's concept of transference–countertransference and projective identification; in Bion's concept of container–contained and alpha–function and, of course, in Plato's receptacle.

For Whitehead (1929, p. 158), "we perceive other things which are in the world of actualities in the same way as we are". That is to say, we observe other entities in the same way that we observe ourselves for researcher and researched are present in the world in the same manner. By the very fact of observing, one perceives and one is being perceived, that is, patient and therapist are constantly influencing each other. They are inextricably joined in an emotional experience, and the psychoanalytic task is to live through it and comprehend it, so that the therapist can help the patient to become aware of it, thereby giving meaning to his experience and inner world.

Whitehead's view that the ultimate units are momentary events allowed him to affirm both internal and external relations. One may note that when Whitehead is emphasizing process, he seems to be contradicting himself, since at such times he says that there is nothing at an instant. For example, Whitehead (1929, p. 146) states:

> process activity, and change are the matter of fact. At an instant there is nothing ... Thus since there are no instants, conceived as simple primary entities, there is no nature at an instant. Thus all interrelations of matter of fact must involve transition in their essence.

Whitehead solves this paradox through his concept of concrescence. Each occasion of experience is internally related to all prior events, but it is externally related to contemporary and future occasions. Contemporary occasions are those that have their moment of becoming at the same time. Whitehead's technical term for becoming is 'concrescence' which means 'becoming concrete' – "the many become one, and are increased by one" (1929, p. 21). With regard to future occasions, it belongs to each occasion that there will be future occasions because 'anticipation' is a part of each occasion, in the sense that it anticipates that it will exert causal influence on the future, although the actual nature of that influence cannot be known in advance, that is, it is external to the present occasion. A person's present experience, being a distinct event, is not strictly identical with his past or future experience. And thus, the transferential relationship between patient and therapist, as repetitive or seemingly repetitive of the past as it might be, can never be quite the same. Every subjective form is different from any other; no subject feels a given datum in precisely the same manner as any other subject has done. This is even the case when the 'subjects' in question are successive instances of the same person or Self – one does not feel the same datum in the same way that one did a minute ago, if only because the memory of the experience of a minute ago has added itself to what one is feeling now. This is what Whitehead means when he states that "no two actual entities originate from an identical universe, though the differences between the two universes only consist in some actual entities, included in one and not in the other" (1929, pp. 22–23). As a consequence, and as paradoxical as it might sound, repetition, including transferential repetition, always produces newness and difference. It is the repetition itself that signals change. Winnicott speaks of the need to fail our patients in the familiar ways that they were failed (Winnicott, 1963). That is, if the patient felt rejected, abandoned, diminished, ridiculed, ashamed, uncared for, unloved by previous relationships, mainly by that with the parents, he will experience the therapist as rejecting, uncaring, abandoning, etc., but this can never be the exact replica, since in this repetition novelty is enclosed. An act of transference is an act of feeling, and an act of feeling is an encounter – a contingent event, an opening to the outside – rather than an intrinsic predetermined relationship. Feeling changes whatever it encounters, even in the act of 'conforming' to it. This is the reason why feeling is irreducible to cognition – it is not anything that one already knows. Every experience, thought included, is a process of being affected. What has already been felt, selected and determined – the very process of selection and determination is the feeling itself – is at the same time an 'inheritance' from the past and a 'fresh creation'.

For Whitehead, feeling – "blind emotion" – rather than cognition, is the basis of all experience, and "apart from experiences of subjects there is nothing, nothing, nothing, bare nothingness" (Whitehead, 1929, p. 167). This suggests that experience can only be organized from within subjective feeling. "Emotions are intensified, and experiences made richer, when incompatibilities, instead of being excluded – negatively prehended – are transformed into contrasts that can be positively integrated within a greater complexity of order" (Ibid., p. 100), which by no means means static perfection. Experience is always able to surprise us.

The patient begins her session in her usual manner, with a complaint. Today her main complaint is "her lack of a place in this world". She relates an episode which has taken place on her way to the session.

She has commuted on a crowded bus, but was lucky enough to get a seat. A young woman on crutches boards the bus, but no one is moving. After a few minutes hesitation, the patient offers her seat to this person. The patient's tone begins to sound superior, self-righteous, arrogant and I begin to feel irritated by the way that she feels that such a small gesture makes her a really good person. I said that perhaps she was communicating to me something of what she feels I do not offer her, or deprive her of, and how angry that might make her feel. It is as if she can be generous, but I cannot, which immediately places her, in her mind, in an elevated position in relationship to me. The patient's response is that the young woman in the bus, unlike herself, is visible to the world, in the sense that she gets sympathy and responses from others (note that nobody got up and offered their seat to the young woman on crutches, except for the patient, but the way she seems to feel the situation is as if every one had been helpful to the woman). I said that she sounded bitter that other people seemed to get more attention and care than herself, and asked if she felt that was also true in relationship to me, and what she imagined was my preferential treatment of other patients. She began to cry, and said that she thought of me as caring and fair. After a few minutes, I said that maybe what she was trying to communicate was how her suffering is not being seen outside the walls of the consulting room, in the sense that she is not 'on crutches', and her 'disability', being an emotional one, is not obvious to the world. This opened up our dialogue, and the patient spoke passionately about how nobody knows what it is like to be her: miserable, lonely, vindictive, toxic, poisonous, guilty ...

During the last few sessions, the patient's suicidal ideation – a recurrent pattern – has been increasing, and I feel concerned that she might act on it. During this time, we have been openly speaking about her desire 'to end it all', and about her fantasies as to how to go about it. Her desire to make people suffer, including me, by such a violent act, has been meticulously explored. She both rejoices and agonizes about the impact that this could have on others, particularly family members, from whom she is estranged. Her sadism, sadomasochism, sense of entitlement and the accompanying feeling that she 'deserves nothing', not even the right to exist, play an important part in our discussions. At times, I observe and interpret an idealization on my patient's part, that she can have more 'value' dead than alive, in the sense that she will be 'seen' and 'remembered'. Certainly she will never be indifferent again, as well as being 'immortal'. It is difficult to maintain the psychoanalytic disposition, and continue to explore and work through whatever emerges in our discussions, under such duress. My feelings seem to oscillate between warm feelings, sympathy and empathy towards a very distressed patient, and irritation, annoyance, and anger for being placed under such burden of responsibility.

In our previous session, I said to her that it is important for her to communicate the precariousness of her situation, and how she feels 'at the edge' – despondent, hopeless, hapless, helpless, in despair. She nodded. In a calm, poised voice, the patient spoke of her fears of taking antidepressants. Surprisingly, astonishingly, she spoke of the value she placed on her therapy, in being listened to, in being taken seriously, and in being able to be in touch with her feelings. She did not want medication which could mascarade her real problems. I agreed with her, in that the underlying issues needed to continue to be worked through, but insisted that, perhaps at this point in time, we could also think of how she could be best helped with her symptoms, particularly her increased suicidal ideation. The conversation continued in an honest and moving manner. We became emotionally closer than we had been for a long time. Most likely, this is what my patient had needed from me, that is, my full care and attention, but she did not know how to ask – 'find her place', or 'have a right to exist', and, instead, her greed and envious attacks often spoiled our dialogues, and, I, on my part, had not 'seen' my patient in the way that she needed to be seen.

I brought these ideas into the open via an interpretation. The positive feeling between us intensified and gained in depth. By the end of the session, she said that she would book an appointment with her GP, but, also, that her feelings were real and belonged to her, and how she would not change that for the world. I was filled with emotion and respect for the patient – she was feeling very depressed, suicidal, but she had learnt to respect and value her own feelings.

This clinical material serves to illustrate how a session which starts in a predictable way, in this case with a complaint of one sort or another, has moved into realms which neither of us could have envisaged at the beginning. It is true that the sense of 'same old, same old', including feeling-tone, reproach and theme feels somewhat repetitive and yet, something new and surprising emerges in every session. The transferential feelings are being brought to me from her relationships in the past, but they are never quite the same feelings, and the trajectory is certainly different every time.

For Whitehead, one's experience of actuality involves the perception of 'prehension' itself – prehension meaning a more fundamental way of grasping things – in addition to one's awareness that one's sensory organs are causing one to have certain experiences, as when the therapist is aware that he is seeing a patient by means of his eyes. Such prehension, while presupposed in sensory perception, is itself non-sensory. Neither does one see one's brain cells, nor one's eyes, but one does prehend them, and, hence, the data they convey. Another example of this non-sensory perception is the person's prehension of immediately prior moments of his experience, through which he knows the reality of the past, and thus, of time.

Whitehead (1933, pp. 224–225), argues in favour of the ancient thinkers who asked: "What have we experienced?" – in opposition to modern thinkers whose question is: "What can we experience?", with the assumption that this question is identical with the question of "what data are directly provided by the activity of the sense organs?" Whitehead (Ibid., p. 176) insists that "the basis of experience is emotional" and, therefore, the question of how we feel, and what we feel are more fundamental than the epistemological question. This emphasis on feeling leads, in turn, to a new account of affect-laden subjectivity. Most broadly, Whitehead's affect theory places aesthetics – rather than ontology (Heidegger) or ethics (Levinas) – at the centre of philosophical enquiry. Aesthetics is the mark of what Whitehead calls our concern for the world, and for entities in the world.

The question of what it is that the patient and therapist are experiencing in a given session, and of how are they experiencing it, are the main psychoanalytic concerns, as well. To feel something is to be affected by something, and the way that the feeling entity is affected, or changed, is the very content of what is felt.

Everything that happens in the universe is in some sense an episode of feeling, even the "actual occasions in so called 'empty-space' discovered by modern physics" (Whitehead, 1929, p. 177). Overall, there is "a hierarchy of categories of feeling" (Ibid., p. 166), from the "wavelengths of vibrations" of subatomic physics (Ibid., p. 163), to the finest subtleties of human subjective experience. But in every case, phenomena are felt, and grasped as modes of feeling, before they can be cognized and categorized. In this way, Whitehead posits feeling as a basic condition of experience, relational and transitional. If perceptual experience is equated with sensory perception, then man has no perceptual experience of causation, the actual world, or the past. There can be neither religious nor numinous experience in the sense of a direct awareness of a divine reality. There can be no perceptual experience of ideals, or hopes, or future.

This idea of non-sensory perception is central to Whitehead's prehensive doctrine of perception, and it is also crucial to psychoanalytic understanding, for the therapist deals with the immediacy of the experience with his patients, which encompasses transference and countertransference feelings, including actual physical feelings, passions, fears, hopes, dreams, phantasies, etc. In short, more often than not, the therapist deals with the unseen, the untouched, the unsaid, the invisible ... but ever so intensively felt. Therefore, the term prehension can be used to refer to what therapists do in psychoanalytic sessions, that is, to refer to a mode of taking account of other things that could be either sensory or non-sensory. Sensory perception, rather than being man's basic mode of perception, is a mixed mode which involves two pure modes. One of these pure modes is representational immediacy, the other is called 'perception in the mode of causal efficacy'. Whitehead's name for this full-fledged sensory perception is 'perception in the mode of symbolic reference'. The point of this name is that the data from one mode are used as symbols to refer to, and hence interpret, the other mode.

The psychoanalytic process could be said to be a symbolic activity, where two people engage on a process of discovery, and where symbolism and imagery are perhaps the only real thing, forever pointing beyond itself towards something as yet unknown.

Whitehead's Ontology

Following on from Whitehead, the process of becoming can be understood as explained by the 'ontological principle', or the 'principle of efficient causation'. Whitehead (1929, p. 84) puts it thus: "Sound metaphysics is to exhibit final and efficient causes in their proper relation to each other". At the root of Whitehead's efforts to fulfil this task was the doctrine that ultimate individuals of which the world is composed are momentary occasions of experience. Each occasion begins as an open window to the past, into which rush causal influences from the past world. This reception of efficient causation constitutes what Whitehead calls the 'physical pole' of the occasion of experience. A 'physical feeling' is here defined to be the feeling of another actuality, and the physical and the mental are intertwined. Locke and Descartes conceive the sensa as purely mental conditions to the facts of physical nature. Both philosophers conceive the physical world as in essential independence of the mental world, though the two worlds have ill-defined accidental relationships – physical/mental duality. According to the philosophy of organism of Whitehead, physical and mental operations are inextricably intertwined; also one finds the sensa functioning as forms participating in the vector prehensions of one occasion by another; and finally in tracing the origin of presentational immediacy, one finds mental operations transmuting the functions of sensa, so as to transfer them from being participants in causal prehensions, into participants in presentational prehensions. But, throughout the whole story, the sensa are participating in nature as much as anything else. It is the function of mentality to modify the physical participation of external objects: the case of presentational prehensions is only one conscious example. The whole doctrine of mentality is that it is a modifying agency.

With the physical pole so constituted, the occasions window is closed, as it were, while the occasion has its 'mental pole' during which it exercises final causation, in the sense of self-determination. In other words, the occasion of experience decides, precisely how to form itself out of the influences it received. In exercising final causation the process is aiming at a goal, an ideal.

These Whiteheadian ideas are most pertinent to psychoanalytic work, for not only are they at the heart of experiences with patients the therapist is trying to understand, but they also reconcile psychoanalytic and analytic traditions. That is to say, they bring together the Freudian 'efficient' causes – personal past experiences of the individual – and the Jungian 'goal' or final causation. The 'why?' and the 'what for?' questions are united in a meaningful event: experience, and neither can do without the other, both have to be grasped simultaneously. What is more, influence from past experiences – personal and collective, conscious and unconscious – is accepted, but not determinism, for the efficient cause carries with it a final one. In other words, influence and freedom are mutually inclusive in any given experience. The past, the present and the future are joined in a momentary glimpse. The efficient causation is the past influencing the present and the future, and the final causation is action directed towards a goal. This goal, or objective aim, is not primarily intellectual; it is the lure for feeling. The concrescence absorbing the derived data into immediate privacy consists in merging the data with ways of feeling. But the how of feeling, though it is germane to the data, is not fully determined by the data. "Feelings are 'vectors', for they feel what is *there*, and transform it into what is *here*" (Whitehead, 1929, p. 87).

Another important feature of Whitehead's cosmology is the idea that each actual entity exists in two modes, that is, existence has two types of value. It exists first as a subject of experience, in which mode it prehends prior experiences and, then, it makes a self-determining response to them, and, after existing as a subject, its subjectivity perishes; it then exists as an object for subsequent subjects. Thus, perpetual perishing means perpetual oscillation; actual entities 'perpetually perish' subjectively, but are immortal objectively. Actuality in perishing acquires objectivity, while it loses subjective immediacy – it loses the final causation, and it acquires efficient causation. While it is a subject enjoying experience, an actual occasion has intrinsic value: value for itself. When it becomes an object for others, it has extrinsic value. It cannot have both kinds of value at the same time.

These Whiteheadian notions are relevant to psychoanalytic work, for the therapist not only needs to be in the experience with his patients, but he also needs to objectify the experience, in order to discuss it, explore it, and understand it – live concepts are living experience. Based on the analytic experience and objectification of it, the therapist is in a better position to abstract, speculate and form new theories which, in turn, enable further progress in psychoanalytic understanding.

Only individual occasions can have intrinsic value: "the percipient occasion is its own standard of actuality" (Whitehead, 1929, p. 145), but anything can be prehended – an individual experience, a temporarily ordered society of occasions, or an aggregation of occasions – can have extrinsic value. Whitehead (Ibid., p. 36) speaks of how subject becomes object, and thereby transcends itself. He says: "There is nothing which belongs merely to the privacy of feeling of one individual actuality". All origination is private, but what has thus been originated publicly pervades the world. In other words, an occasion of experience, in being objectified for others – and oneself – thereby transcends itself, and "such transcendence is self-revelation" (Ibid., p. 227). One's emotions, attitudes and thoughts are known as soon as they are knowable, and to the extent that they can be known. For Whitehead, process or creativity is the ultimate reality, which implies that to be an actuality is necessarily to be a process of creative synthesis, so that any world would of necessity be a world of process. Psychotherapists sometimes can lose sight of the process of creative synthesis that the work entails and, instead, they focus too eagerly on the patient's progress, as opposed to psychoanalytic process.

The only thing one has direct inside knowledge of is his own perceiving, or, more generally, his own experiencing. This is his own and only inside knowledge of actual experience – of what it is like to be an actuality. The enduring Self is a temporarily ordered society of occasions of experience, of momentary events, and each event is an experience with memory and anticipation.

If memory and anticipation are inextricably linked in every experience, and if what is unique about species and what makes one fully human is long-term expectation and memory, it is difficult to endorse Bion's view regarding the necessity to approach the session with 'no memory or desire'. And yet, the therapist needs to do so, in order not to pre-empt the immediacy of the experience with knowledge from the past and expectations for the patient's future – if the therapist is to allow for an opportunity for reverie and for the state of 'not-knowing', and to allow for whatever needs to emerge to come forth. In short, if the therapist is to meet the patient where he or she is at that very moment in time. It would seem that, as it is often the case in psychoanalytic work, holding in mind the paradox, as opposed to polarize, dichotomize, split up or place oneself in a position of 'either/ or', is important, in order to carry out the psychoanalytic opus in an open-ended manner. This is what Jung demonstrates throughout, for in his encounters with the unconscious, he struggles between doubt and desire.

Each occasion of experience arises out of its relations to former occasions of experience, and then contributes itself to later occasions. Each moment of experience is a microcosm, taking into itself, at least to some slight degree, all prior events. For the momentary Self to realize its true nature is to realize that it is akin to all other things, but, is this the true nature of the Self? The implication is that the Self's nature is transition, since at an instant there is nothing; that is, an instant is only a way of grouping process, activity and change – 'the matter of fact' – then, there are no instants conceived as primary entities and therefore, no nature at an instant. Thus, all the interrelations of matters of fact must involve transition in their essence; change is constant. Every realization implies implication in the creative advance: matter of fact is transcendental. In other words, things, human beings, the Self, strive not to persist in their own being, but rather to become other than they were, to make some alteration to the 'data' that they received. An entity's satisfaction is not based in persisting in its own being, but in achieving difference as novelty: in introducing something new into the world.

Whitehead differs from Kant in seeing subjective unity as an ongoing process, rather than as a fixed form, and in describing this process as a matter of feeling, rather than as one of thinking. While for Kant, the formal unity of the subject is given once and for all, for Whitehead, this unity has to be produced afresh at every moment – since the subject itself must be produced afresh at every moment. This means that the subjective unity is not the framework of experience (as it is for Kant), but rather a consequence of experience, and that is what opens the door to novelty. Every achievement of unity is something that has never existed before, something different, something radically new.

> An actual occasion is a novel entity diverse from any entity in the many, which it unifies ... The ultimate metaphysical principle is the advance from disjunction to conjunction, creating a novel entity other than the entities given in disjunction ... The many become one, and are increased by one.
>
> (Whitehead, 1929, p. 21)

There is no permanent unity, but only continual transition to unity. The therapist could not carry out psychoanalytic work if he did not implicitly or explicitly endorse this view: man is a process involved in a process beyond himself.

Plato's Ontology Is Akin to Whitehead's

Similarly, in *Timaeus*, Plato (1965) states that the world of time "is a process of becoming and perishing and never really is". Completion is the perishing of immediacy: "it never really is". However, Plato also believed (vaguely, inconsistently) that what is fully real is a realm of eternal and unchangeable forms: eternal forms that exist independently of the physical world. Plato's recurring fascination was the distinction between ideal forms and everyday experience, and how it played out both for individuals and for societies. At times, it would seem that Plato, like Descartes, gave priority to being over becoming, but nothing is that clear-cut with Plato, and the primacy of becoming comes across throughout Plato's writings both in its content and in its form, in the sense that the dialogues themselves are explorations, a flux of ideas and feelings which are forever evolving, being both found and created through conversations – with himself and with his interlocutors – as opposed to being opinions held in advance. In other words, for Whitehead, as for Plato, and for the psychotherapists, the subject arises in and through experience and insight, that is, through the exploration, struggle, doubt and conflict involved in the dialectic process. Further, for Plato, the process of the actual world has been conceived as a real incoming of forms into real potentiality, issuing into the real togetherness, which is the real thing. In Plato's *Timaeus*, the creation of the world is the incoming of a type of order establishing a cosmic epoch. For both Plato and Whitehead, the receptacle as described in *Timaeus* is the middle ground between being and becoming. It is the realm 'within' and 'between' what is stable and what changes. In the interplay between these two, identity emerges as that which remains amidst the flux of events. In order to see identity, one needs to see identity in change. The receptacle for both Plato and Whitehead is the stable ground that welcomes all the changes and remains permanent in its nature. For both thinkers the receptacle is the matrix of all becoming, the underlying matrix that enables the unfolding of that process which is reality.

It is as if there is no stone that Plato left unturned, so to speak, and no thought which man is struggling with today that he did not attempt to elucidate. In Whitehead's (1929, p. 39) words: "The safest general characterization of the European philosophical tradition is that it consists of a series of footnotes to Plato". Thus, Plato wondered about the nature of being, he asked: "What does it mean for anything at all to be?" He especially wanted to argue that ideas have being. Thus, in the *Sophist*, Plato (1997) established one of the cornerstones of all Western thought by defining the nature of being. His notion is that anything that possesses any sort of power to affect another, if only for a moment, however trifling the cause and however slight the effect, has real existence. He therefore holds the view that the definition of being is simply power. For Plato there is no being without power, and power should be understood as both the ability to affect, and the ability to be affected. In this sense, psychoanalytic sessions are powerful, for certainly both participants are powerfully affected and changed. This notion is closely linked to Jung's (1946) psychic infection in the therapeutic relationship, and to Bion's (1965) transformation in O.

The problem with the notion of power, however, arises when only one side of its dual meaning is taken into account, mainly the ability to affect, while the ability to be affected is largely viewed as a defeat or weakness. It is not man's power to remain unaffected, or even the power to control others, that makes his life richer and more valuable; it is his amazing capacity to be affected by the incredible richness and complexity of the relational web in which he lives. His capacity for pain and pleasure, his physical senses, his appreciation of beauty, his openness to ideas and feelings, and his ability to learn and to adapt is what makes him human, and what enables the emphatic and empathic impact of psychoanalytic encounters. The deeper the therapist gets psychologically and emotionally engaged with his patients, that is, the deeper he gets into the cauldron together, the more the power to affect and to be affected emerges. However, both for Plato and the psychotherapists, there is a crucial difference between the kind of weakness that makes a person vulnerable to being controlled by others, and the strength that enables him to be active and open to the world around him. There is a vital equal difference between the power to control others, while shutting them out of one's life, and the power to engage the lives of others in ways that enrich them. The latter is the privileged situation between patient and therapist that the psychoanalytic encounters enable.

Whitehead recognized the importance of the language of being, but found deeper wisdom and greater clarity in a vision of the world as becoming: a relational process (although, of course, being and power, and the power of being, also involves a relational process of a different nature: a relationship between two people). Whitehead (1929, p.25), states that how an actual entity, an event, becomes, constitutes what that actual entity is; its 'being' is constituted by its 'becoming'. This is the principle of process. An entity is actual when it has significance for itself.

It seems that stability is a relative matter in the flow of experience. Many experiences and personality features change and still leave one with a clear sense that one is still oneself. But sometimes, massive changes, such as the patients' traumatic experiences or illnesses, including brain damage, Alzheimer's or after dementia can create such change that he is not recognisable to oneself or others. It is as if, if one takes away all these qualities, there is simply nothing left. Man is a bundle of qualities, and a dynamic bundle at that. Of course, some qualities in that bundle are more persistent than others, but there is no unchanging 'Self', no mental substance that endures unchanged through the changes of qualities, or that exist independently of those qualities, so as to remain if they were all taken away. At this point, Whitehead is closer to the Buddhist view of 'no-Self', or *anatman*, and to the Jungian (and Hume's) view of 'nothing at the centre of the Self', than to the Hindu view of *atman*, as an indestructible Self, or the Christian one, of an equally indestructible soul.

In Plato's *Apology* (1977) (note that Socrates does not apologize for anything, but actually defends himself via speech in a legal proceeding – this is the Greek meaning of Apology – against the charge of breaking the law against 'impiety' – for offending the Olympian gods (Zeus, Apollo, etc), which carries the death penalty), Socrates argues that they can take away his life but not his soul, for his soul is immortal.

References

Bion, W. R. (1965). Transformations. *Seven Servants*. New York: Jason Aronson, 1977.

James, W. (1912). *Essays on Radical Empiricism*. Lincoln, NE: University of Nebraska Press, 1966.

Jung, C. G. (1946). Translated by R. F. C. Hull. *The Psychology of the Transference*. London: Routledge, 1983.

Plato. (1965). Apology. *Timaeus and Critias*. Edited by J. M. Cooper and D. S. Hutchison, translated by D. Lee. London: Penguin.

Plato. (1977). Apology. *Plato Complete Works*. Edited by J. M. Cooper and D. S. Hutchison. Indianapolis: Hackett Publishing.

Plato. (1997). The sophists. *Plato Complete Works*. Edited by J. M. Cooper and D. S. Hutchison. Indianapolis: Hackett Publishing.

Plato. (1997). Letter VIII. *Plato Complete Works*. Edited by J. M. Cooper and D. S. Hutchison. Indianapolis: Hackett Publishing.

Plato. (1997). The laws. *Plato Complete Works*. Edited by J. M. Cooper and D. S. Hutchison. Indianapolis: Hackett Publishing.

Whitehead, A. N. (1929). *Process and Reality*. Corrected ed., D. R. Griffin and D. W. Sherburne, Eds. New York: The Free Press, 1985.

Whitehead, A. N. (1933). *Adventure of Ideas*. New York: The Free Press, 1967.

Whitehead, A. N. (1938). *Modes of Thought*. New York: The Free Press, 1968.

Winnicott, D. W. (1963). *The Maturational Process and the Facilitating Environment*. London: Karnac, 1990.

Chapter 7

Whitehead and Heraclitus
Permanence, Flux and Novelty

Introduction

Whitehead's view regarding the flow of experience, and the Self as a process forever becoming, is akin to the notion of Heraclitus's River, for man is the flow of his experience. Heraclitus (535–475 BC) states: "No man steps in the same river twice, for it is not the same river and he is not the same man". Man's soul, his mind, his psyche is that river, that stream, or that flux. His sense of identity in that flux comes from memory and anticipation. Once again, it is difficult to advocate Bion's recommendation of approaching every session with 'no memory or desire' from this standpoint.

Both Whitehead and Plato follow Heraclitus's dictum. However, Whitehead adds to Heraclitus's dictum by describing not only fluency in being and experience, but also two kinds of fluency. In psychoanalytic work, we are witness to the flux and the permanence of the human mind; there is an energetic flow of symbolic resonance. The ego as mind sees things in its own image, but analysis is seen as a place of birth and growth (Jung), where two individuals – patient and therapist – are experientially together in their solitude.

Man's Continuity and Novelty

There is a chain of experience out of which the individual arises, in each moment. He feels that that is his own past, and he anticipates that the decisions he makes in the present will shape a series of future experiences that will, in turn, be created out of this historical chain. The cumulative flow of psychological experience, including the individual's own decisions shaping that series, is what the individual is: it is

DOI: 10.4324/9781003261841-8

his mind, psyche, soul or Self. In this respect, it is not only that man cannot step into the same river twice, it is, actually, that he himself is the river, the stream in constant flux. Man has a sense of Self because of this continuity. He arises out of the past, out of his relationships with the world, with himself and with others, and enjoys a moment present that includes participation of future experiences. That moment becomes and perishes and gives birth to a new moment, which recreates man with both continuity and novelty. Novelty is essential for man's survival. If one never changed, one would die – though the individual is constantly changing and he also dies. Novelty is the root of life. Life is a balance between order and novelty. In that flux of experiences and decisions, a certain persistent personality is shaped. The paradox of enduring order and chaos, absence and presence, safety and novelty is most pertinent to psychoanalytic sessions, for patients seek therapy in order to change – at least some aspects of their personality – and, simultaneously, defend against change as the most feared of all potential catastrophes. Freud (1920) was well aware of this fact, to the extent that he postulated the 'compulsion to repeat' as the ultimate fact – that is to say, more funda-mental than pleasure seeking. For Whitehead, however, becoming is the ultimate fact underlying all others. Whitehead refers to this ultimate fact, this ultimate character, shared by all actual things, as creativity. "Creativity is the principle of novelty" (1929, p. 21). For Whitehead, creativity is the universal of universals characterizing ultimate matter of fact. It is that ultimate principle by which the many, which are the uni-verse disjunctively, become the one actual occasion, which is the uni-verse conjunctively. It lies in the nature of things that the many enter into complex unity. Whitehead (Ibid., p. 104) reminds us that the pri-mary meaning of life is the capacity for novel reactions, because life is essentially "a bid for freedom". In the case of those actualities whose immediate experience is most completely open to man (his own experi-ence of self-creativity) is the foundation of his experience of responsi-bility – of self-approved or self-reproach, of freedom, of emphasis – "It governs the whole of human life" (Ibid., p. 47).

In this respect, Whitehead is in agreement with Plato, in that "the definition of being is simply power", and every actual entity has the power to create itself within the limits provided by the actual world. The self-creativity includes the capacity to take what is given and create its own subjective aim. An actual entity, an event, is a subject of its own experience – it is a self-creative drop of feeling. When an actual entity completes its process of becoming "this final unity is termed the 'satisfaction'" (Ibid., p. 212) – it achieves its objective aim. While it becomes, it is a subject of its own feeling. Once it has become and perishes, it becomes raw material to be prehended by future actual entities – what it prehends are the feelings. It is no longer a subject for itself; it becomes an object.

Plato's Eternal Forms, Whitehead's Eternal Objects and Jung's Archetypes

Whitehead preserved Plato's Forms. He called them 'eternal objects'. This concept is also akin to Jung's archetypes: potentialities. However, Whitehead rejected Plato's proposal that those forms constituted ulti-mate reality. For Whitehead, the world of becoming and perishing is more fundamentally real. Psychoanalytic thinking too endorses this view, since the therapist's experience is that patients experience stale-mate, but also many, varied, and unexpected changes through the psy-choanalytic relationship and discourse. Potentiality, for Whitehead, is always something more, and other, than mere possibility. Alongside events or actual entities, Whitehead also posits what he calls "eternal objects". These are "pure potentials" (1929, p. 22), or "potentials for the process of becoming" (Ibid., p. 29). If actual entities are singular "occasions" of becoming, then eternal objects provide "the qualities and relations" (Ibid., p. 191) that enter into, and help to define, these occa-sions. When "the potentiality of an eternal object is realized in a parti-cular actual entity, it contributes to the definiteness of that actual entity" (Ibid., p. 23): it gives it a particular character. Eternal objects, thus, take on something of the role of universals (Ibid., p. 48, 158), predicates (Ibid., p.86), Platonic Forms (Ibid., p. 44) and Ideas (Ibid., pp. 52, 149), played in older metaphysical systems. However, for Whitehead, a "con-crete particular fact" cannot simply "be built up out of universals", it is more the other way round: universals, or "things which are eternal" can and must be abstracted from "things that are temporal" (Ibid., p. 40). Eternal objects cannot be conceived by themselves in the absence of the empirical and temporal entities that they inform, in the same way that an archetype needs to become personified/embodied.

> Eternal objects, therefore, are neither a priori logical structures,
> nor Platonic essences, nor constitutive rational ideas. They are
> adverbial, rather than substantive; they determine and express how
> actual entities relate to one another, take one another up, and
> enter into each other's constitutions.
>
> (Ibid., pp. 148–149)

Affects or emotions are eternal objects; and so are 'contrasts, or patterns', or anything else that can "express a manner of relatedness between other 'eternal objects'" (Ibid., p. 144). Eternal objects are abstractions that nevertheless (in contrast to Platonic Forms) can only be encountered with experience, when they are 'selected' and 'felt' by particular actual occasions – this is also Poincaré's (1952) 'selected fact'.

Whitehead's use of the word 'eternal' may seem controversial, in the context of a philosophy grounded in events, becomings, and continual change and novelty. Indeed, as if acknowledging this, he remarks that "if the term 'eternal objects' is disliked, the term 'potentials' would be suitable, instead" (1929, p. 149). Having said that, Whitehead himself prefers to retain the appellation 'eternal objects'. This is precisely because he seeks to reject the Platonic separation between eternity and time, the binary opposition that sets a higher world of permanence and perfection – a static, spiritual heaven – against an imperfect lower world of flux. The two instead must continually interpenetrate; for permanence can be snatched only out of flux, and the passing moment can find its adequate intensity only by its submission to permanence. Actual entities continually perish, but the relations between them, or the patterns that they make, tend to recur or endure. Thus, it is not 'substance' which is permanent, but 'form', and even forms do not subsist absolutely, but continuously "suffer changing relations" (Ibid., p. 29).

When Whitehead says that forms as well as substances, or eternal objects as well as actual entities, must be accepted as real, he is arguing very much in the spirit of the radical empiricism of Willian James (1842–1910). For James, "experience is the sole criterion of reality, we live in a world of pure experience" (James, 1912/1966, pp. 39–91).

Classical empiricism (as opposed to radical empiricism) has great difficulty in making sense of relations, as well as emotions, contrasts and patterns, and all the other phenomena that Whitehead classifies as 'eternal objects'. Since these cannot be recognized as 'things', or as direct 'impressions of sensation', they are neglected to the status of mental fictions: habits, derivatives, secondary qualities and so on. But James says that in a world of pure experience, 'relations' are every bit as real as 'things', "the relations that connect experiences must themselves be experienced relations, and any kind of relation experienced must be accounted as 'real' as anything else in the system" (Ibid., p. 42). Whitehead argues by the same logic, that is to say, that eternal objects must be accounted as real as the actual entities which they qualify, and which selects them, include them, and incarnate them. Eternal objects are real because they are themselves 'experienced relations', or primordial elements of experience.

"An eternal object is always a potentiality for actual entities, but in itself, as conceptually felt, it is neutral as to the fact of its physical ingression in any particular entity of the temporal world" (Whitehead, 1929, p. 44). At the same time, every event, every actual occasion, involves the actualization of these mere potentialities. Each actual entity is determined in what Whitehead calls ingression of specific eternal objects into it. The term 'ingression' refers to the particular mode in which the potentiality of an eternal object is realized in a particular actual entity, contributing to the definiteness of that actual entity (Ibid., p. 23). Each actual entity creates itself, in a process of decision, by making a selection among the potentialities offered to it by eternal objects. The concrescence of each actual entity involves the rejection of some eternal objects, and the active "entertainment", or "admission into feeling" of others (Ibid., p. 188). Consequently, by a kind of circular process, the eternal objects thus admitted or entertained, serve to define and determine the entity that selected them – by offering themselves for actualization, and by determining the very entities that select and actualize them, eternal objects play a transcendental, quasi-causal role in the constitution of the actual world. The actual and the potential reciprocally determine one another for Whitehead.

Whitehead also explains the difference and the relation between the eternal objects and actual entities by noting that the former "can be dismissed" at any moment, whereas the latter always "have to be felt" (Ibid., p. 239). This is similar to Bion's (1965) notion that 'O has to be been'. Potentialities are optional; they may or may not be fulfilled, but actualities cannot be avoided, and yet, every time, in every experience, one potentiality or another will be part of the actuality. Indeed, "an actual entity in the actual world of a subject must enter into the concrescence of that subject's simple causal feeling, however vague, trivial and submerged" (Whitehead, 1929, p. 239). An actual entity can, in fact, be rejected or excluded, by the process of what Whitehead called a negative prehension: "the definite exclusion of (a given) item from positive contribution to the subject's own real internal constitution" (Ibid., p. 41). But even this is a sort of backhander that cannot just be ignored. Even the negative prehension of an entity is a positive fact with its emotional subjective form (Ibid., pp.41–42). In other words, the negative prehension is negative in one respect and positive in another, inasmuch as the individual's negative capability is negative in what it is not, and positive in what it enables.

An actual entity has causal efficacy, because in itself it is entirely determined, in the sense that it is empirically "given", and this "givenness" means necessity (Ibid., pp. 42–43). "Once actual entities have completed their process, once the ingression of eternal objects into them has been fixed, they are devoid of all indetermination ... they are complete and determinate ... devoid of all indecision" (Ibid., p. 29). Every event culminates in a "stubborn matter of fact" (Ibid., p. 239), a state of affairs that has no potential left, and that cannot be otherwise than it is. An event consists precisely in this movement from potentiality (and indeterminacy) into actuality (and complete determination). The process of actualization follows a trajectory from the mere, disinterested (aesthetic) "envisagement of eternal objects" (Ibid., p. 44) to a pragmatic interest in some of these objects, and their incorporation within "stubborn fact which cannot be evaded" (Ibid., p. 43). In the course of fully determining itself, an actual entity perishes, and subsists only as a "datum" for other entities to prehend in their turn. An eternal object, on the other hand, is not exhausted by the event into which it ingresses, or which includes it; it "never loses its 'accent' of potentiality" (Ibid., p. 239) – it remains available for other events, other actualizations; this is another mark of the transcendental. Eternal objects never disappear; they are "indispensable conditions" that cannot be grasped outside of the actualities that they condition, and that incarnate them, but they cannot be reduced to those actualities either, and cannot be contained within them. Eternal objects are not actual, but they haunt the actual – they subsist, like spectres, outside of their ingression and actualizations, and according to a different temporal logic than that of the "specious present of the percipient" (Ibid., p.169), the present in which things happen. This outside, this extra-being, this space without "simple location" (Ibid., p. 137), this time in which the present continuously divides into past and future is the realm of the transcendental.

Akin to Jung's question, the fundamental question that Whitehead asks and seeks to answer with his transcendental arguments about eternal objects, and Jung about archetypes are these: How is it that there is always something new? How are novelty and change possible? How can one account for a future that is different from, and not merely predetermined by the past? Behind all of these is the question with which I began: What is an event? These are the questions of psychoanalytic enquiry, as well.

Whitehead and Plato on Creativity

Whitehead's interest, like Plato's, lies in the dissolution of old certainties, in order to create doubt. He is actively engaged in working out new ways of thinking, new ways to exercise the faculty of wonder. He does not see any point in returning to man's ultimate beginnings – he is interested in creation, the new, that is, becoming rather than being. In a similar way to Jung, Whitehead urges man to work with the challenges of the present, to negotiate them. How, he asks, can man and culture's incessant repetition and recycling, issue forth as something genuinely new and different?

Openness to the immediacy of the experience with patients is also where the therapist needs to be in, and work with, and then, through that, to find the creative spark, the flux, the movement from the stalemate that frequently patients find themselves in, in the form of the patient's neurosis and defence mechanisms, towards something new, different, fluid, transformative and transcendental. Both Whitehead (1929) and Winnicott (1971), are talking of creativity not as a successful and acclaimed creation such as a piece of art, music, writing, etc., but rather as something which refers to the whole attitude, to subjective and external reality, to the person engaging with the

problems of ordinary living and the universals of individual development in a given environment. This creativity belongs to being alive,
and living creatively means being in touch with both the subjective
world and with the creative approach to fact. In this sense, everything
that happens is creative, except in so far as the individual is ill, or is
hampered by ongoing environmental factors which stifle his creative
processes. If this happens, compliance ensues and a sense of futility for
the individual who cannot suffer his problems, but only feel the pain.
This state of being or frame of mind is often associated with the idea
that nothing matters, and that life is not worth living. The psychoanalytic task when one encounters these difficulties in a patient might
be to bear with him, to help him to face his conflicts, that is, to help
him to suffer his losses, so that a possibility may open up for him to
unshackle the creative impulse, and to feel that, all difficulties included, life is worth living. In some patients, one observes that all that is
real, personal, original, genuine, creative, that is, all that matters is
hidden, and gives no sign of its existence, but it is equally true that the
creative impulse itself cannot be destroyed utterly. It might be one
psychoanalytic task to recover it and restore it, towards flux, movement, creative spark, which is new, different, transformative and
transcendental. Creativity, like anything else in human nature, must
keep moving and evolving. Heraclitus's river is always in flux.

In Plato's *Cratylus*, Socrates states: "I seem to see Heraclitus spout-
ing some ancient bits of wisdom that Homer also tells us – wisdom as
old as the days of Cronus and Rhea".

Hermogenes asked: "What are you referring to?" Socrates replied:
"Heraclitus says that 'everything gives way and nothing stands fast', and
likening the things that are, to the flowing of a river, he says that you
cannot step into the same river twice". Socrates also tells Hermogenes:
"The nature of things themselves are never stable, but flowing and
moving, full of every sort of motions and constant coming into being".
Socrates continues: "Wisdom is the understanding of motion and flow.
Knowledge indicates that a worthwhile soul follows the movement of
things. Comprehension, that one comprehends, that one knows means
that the soul journeys together with things".

Through psychoanalytic encounters, the therapist endeavours to
acquire wisdom, knowledge, comprehension, meaning, to get to know

himself, and to enable patients to live a worthwhile life creatively. But the aporia, the claustrum, the inability to flow and move on is everything that hinders movement and action. This stalemate is the thing/place/aspect which therapists frequently need to work with/through, with patients. At such times, the river of life is no longer a flowing stream, but it has become a festering pond, so to speak.

In Plato's *Parmenides* (1997), one reads that the instant seems to signify something such that changes occur. The instant lurks between motion and rest – being in no time at all.

In the *Laws X* (1997), the Athenian in conversation with Clinias opines that the soul, by virtue of its motions, stirs into movement everything in the heavens and on earth, and on the sea. The names of the motions of the soul are: wisdom, reflection, diligence, counsel, opinion true and false, joy and grief, cheerfulness and fear, love and hate … These are the instruments soul uses, whether it cleaves the divine reason and gives everything to an appropriate and successful conclusion, or allies itself with unreason and produces completely opposite results.

For both Plato and Heraclitus, the soul is the source of all emotion. In Plato's *Epinomis* (1997), the Athenian tells Clinias the soul is the cause of the whole cosmos. Similarly, Jung (1957) says that every science is a function of the psyche, and all knowledge is rooted in it. The psyche is the greatest of all cosmic wonders and the sine qua non of the world as an object.

In the *Liber Novus* (*Red Book*, 2009), Jung states that the centre is the goal. The Self is the principle and archetype of orientation and meaning. The Self is the goal of individuation, but this process is not linear, but consists in a circumambulation of Self – mandala as process. The sooner one is flowing in the stream/river, the sooner one finds himself back in the festered pond, which by now is a different one, and so the cycle of life goes on.

In *On Justice* (1997), Socrates states that "the soul is what we think with". In *Letter VII* (1997), Plato tells us that "the soul seems to know not the quality, but the essence". The Athenian states:

Self-generating motion is the source of all motions, and the primary force in both stationary and moving objects, and we shall not be able to avoid the conclusion that it is the most ancient and the most potent of all changes, whereas the change which is produced by something else, and is in turn transmitted to others comes second.

Mrs. R starts her session in her customary manner, that is, by offering a report of her multiple medical appointments for her chronic physical illnesses. All the nuanced details of how many things doctors and nurses get wrong or have missed in their examinations of her are spelled out. I feel the outpouring of negativity and make a transference interpretation as to how she might feel I am failing her. She expresses frustration regarding the slow process and even slower progress of therapy in sorting out her long-standing problems. I acknowledge her frustration and allow for some further expression of it, but I also point out something which I have interpreted many times over the years: that her detailed report of events seems to have a psychological function as a defence mechanism, for it prevents us from dealing with the more pressing, emotional and unconscious problems. Today the report is mainly negative in that she seems to have been wronged by every doctor and nurse, but similarly, when the report seems to go in the opposite direction, the effect is the same. Either way, a long chunk of the session is taken up and avoidance of the real issues ensues. Either way, whether her frustration comes from internal factors or from environmental ones – from other people – her omnipotence is being challenged, that is, nothing feels under her control, and this infuriates her. Thus, her need to control the session. Mrs. R ponders about what I have said and recognizes her incessant talking as a way of keeping me at arms length, and herself also intellectually and emotionally detached from herself. She expands on how she is always busy, occupying every minute of her existence with tasks, duties, chores and "noise" in her head, as a way to keep at bay other more terrifying thoughts and feelings. She then said that the previous week something "clicked" in her mind, prompted by a complaint from her husband. Apparently he had told her that he could no longer bear her outpouring of negative feelings, including dissatisfaction, anger, frustration, etc., on a daily basis – that he could no longer tolerate the tone of her speeches after work, for it made him feel very depressed, helpless and under constant personal attack, even when she appeared to be talking about other people letting her down. Rather than becoming defensive, she reflected on what the other – her husband – was saying, saw his despair for the first time, and decided to change her behaviour. She then said that for the last few days, when she returns home from work, she makes a Herculean effort not to outpour her daily complaints on him and that this has had a major impact in their relationship. She said she felt very happy that she could make a difference to their marriage, but she felt even happier by what she had achieved internally. She struggled to explain what she meant by this, but eventually said that she felt that what she had been doing to her husband for years, with her incessant moaning felt as if she was "vomiting out" into him, and how now she felt more ready to keep it in and digest it. I remarked on the paradox, in the sense that it sounded as if the more of herself she kept inside, the more room she had at her disposal – for feeling and thinking. I also said that for as long as she kept going round and round with all that negativity, not only was there no room for anything else, but perhaps it was also fuelling her rage even further. As if a revelation had come to her, she exclaimed: "That is exactly it!" She continued: "the more I 'vomit' the more empty I feel, and I usually end up feeling bitter and my husband gets angrier and more depressed in listening to me". "Helpless", really, she added. Our dialogue continued and Mrs. R surprised herself in recognizing that her reproaches and laments felt to the listener not just as words, but as daggers, making him feel accused, helpless and guilty, and herself depleted. I made a transferential interpretation regarding the unconscious purpose of using the same evacuative mechanism in our sessions, possibly in order to get rid of her feeling, to stab me with it, and to give me an experience of what it is like being on the receiving end of it, as she was as a child in relationship to her parents. She expanded on it, on how her childhood environment had been a continuous and angry expression of disappointment and frustration by both her parents, and how guilty and angry it made her feel, a sense that it was all her fault.

I feel that our conversation was helpful to her, in the sense of participation in her experience and thinking about it, but I also think that it was the patient herself who reached her own understating about her own predicament. She now knows that the psychoanalytic process takes time, but also that by enduring, reflecting and working through it something shifts internally in her inner world. Now she really knows, for she has experienced it and suffered it, rather than just evacuating it. There is a sense of excitement and achievement in both of us, for something new has emerged. But then, a moment of sadness erupted, not strong enough though to dispel the prior experience, but significant enough to be noted. Mrs. R pondered: "why didn't I realize before the level of venom that I bring to relationships by constant negativity? After all, you have been trying to explore it with me for years. Why do I miss something so simple?" I said: "It needed time to be understood emotionally. Perhaps it is only now that you could hear it, and that you could hear it not from me but from yourself". She agreed and left in a happy mood, and with a sense of value in herself and in what we do together, including a no lesser sense of puzzlement about her discovery and its impact – this time the impact was on herself. I am referring to the positive impact, shift and emotional development of this session, or rather, of the years of work that enabled this session. There is in every session an emotional impact, but not necessarily a growth-promoting one.

Flux Encompasses Permanence and Vice Versa

Following Heraclitus, it is Plato's, Jung's, Whitehead's and the therapist's view that all 'things flow'. However, Whitehead (1929, p. 208) questions: "What sort of things flow?" … "What is the meaning of the 'many' things engaged in this common flux?" Whitehead is also aware that there is a rival notion, antithetical to the former. The other question dwells on the permanence of things – the solid earth, mountains, stones, the Egyptian pyramids, the spirit of man, the seemingly unmovable patient's state of mind. Heraclitus's river is never the same river and simultaneously it is: it is always a river but not the same one. Whitehead (1929, p. 208) quotes the first two lines of a famous hymn which captures a full expression of the union of the two notions in one integral experience:

> Abide with me;
> Fast falls the eventide.

Whitehead (Ibid., p. 338) expounds how in "Fast falls the eventide", ideas fashion themselves round the two notions of permanence and flux. In the inescapable flux there is something that abides; in the overwhelming permanence there is an element that escapes the flux. There is a timelessness in what in its essence is passing. The present moment is fadeless in the lapse of time. Time has lost its character of "perpetual perishing"; it becomes the moving image of eternity. In psychoanalytic sessions, Kronos and Kairos accompany each other. The former signals the 50 minutes of the session, the latter the quality of the experience – both refer to time, but one is chronological time or temporal time, the other is timeless time. The 50 minutes can feel like 50 minutes, like a short breath, or like an eternity – every session is ephemeral and everlasting.

Change is constant, man is part of it. Whitehead (1929, p. 210) adds to Heraclitus's dictum by describing not only fluency, but also two kinds of fluency. One is the concrescence which, in Locke's language is "the real internal constitution of a particular existence". The other kind is the transition from particular existence to particular existence.

In Heraclitus, Plato, Whitehead, Jung and in psychoanalytic work, one is a witness to the flux and the permanence of the human mind; there is an energetic flow of symbolic resonance. The ego as mind sees things in its own image, but therapy is seen as a place of rebirth and all the modes of work represent mandalas, birth places, vessels of birth. There is a richness of mind which consists of mental receptivity, not in accumulation of possessions. This is for Jung 'the perpetual continuation of life', in ritual, such as the ritual of analysis where slaying, dismembering, repairing, symbol formation, transcendental function and rebirth take place. In surviving the analytic experience one is always more than surviving; in thinking one is always thinking more than one thinks; in speaking one is saying more than one says. "In being ourselves, we are more than ourselves" (Whitehead, 1925, p. 23). "More than" is the subject becoming object and the object becoming subject in Whitehead's terms. Man cannot escape his dual reality of becoming and perishing. It is along these lines that Winnicott (1971) describes emotional reality as the process of becoming destroyed because real, and becoming real because destroyed.

Perishing is implicit in becoming and becoming in perishing. If becoming and perishing are split apart, one's present is immediately diminished; together they are conceived with the individual and die with him. Time remembered in man's profound feeling of life, and denial of time in his fear of death are both at the depths of man's being. Man is being lured, allured, seduced, repulsed, incited or dissuaded, and this is part of the process by which he becomes what he is. For Whitehead (1929, p.29), the subject is always also a superject, coming after the process of creation, rather than before. The subject emerges from the world. This process proceeds from objectivity to subjectivity, rather than the other way around. "The external world is a datum, to the subjectivity, whereby there is one individual experience" (Ibid., p.156).

Kant (1781/1966, p. 107) famously writes in the *First Critique of Pure Reason* that "Thoughts without content are empty, intuitions without concepts are blind". This is supposed to mean that intuition and concept must always go together, but in the *Third Critique* he discovers the actuality of contentless thoughts and blind intuitions. Similarly Bion (1997) speaks of thoughts without a thinker – for rational ideas are precisely thoughts that no content can fill; and aesthetic ideas are intuitions that admit of no content. Once one leaves the realm of understanding one discovers a fundamental asymmetry between concepts and intuitions, such as each of them exceeds the power of the other. The active, originary Self, alongside concepts are dispensed with in the *Third Critique*; beauty is felt, rather than comprehended or willed and intuition is decoupled from thought. Thus, Whitehead's ideas are closer to Kant's *Third Critique* than to the first or the second. For Whitehead (1929, p. 156), as for Kant, "in every act of experience there are objects for knowledge,; but, apart from the inclusion of intellectual functioning in the act of experience, there is no knowledge". In other words, although objects of experience can be known, it does not mean that they are known. In fact, cognition or intellectual functioning is often absent in any given experience and thus, 'no knowledge' prevails. The external world as datum enters the being before the mind can think. In *Process and Reality* (1929, pp. 155–156), Whitehead says: "the inclusion of intellectual functioning in the act of experience is in fact quite rare; 'no-knowledge' is by far the more usual one". "Experience is implicit, below consciousness, in our physical feelings" (Ibid., p. 229). These "physical feelings" precede the subject. The subject is solicited by the feeling that comprise it; it only comes to be through these feelings. It is not a substance but a process, and this process is not usually conscious; it only becomes so under exceptional circumstances. This is why Whitehead devalues knowledge, inverting the Kantian notion between subject and object (in the *First Critique*, Kant (1781) states that experience is fundamentally conscious and cognitive), Self and World. From a more psychoanalytic and developmental viewpoint, but akin to Whitehead's understanding, Winnicott states that the object is the subject in the sense of the baby becoming the breast (or mother) through their experience of being. Winnicott (1971) states that however complex the psychology of the sense of Self and of the establishment of an identity which eventually becomes as a baby grows, no sense of Self emerges except on the basis of this relating in the sense of Being. In other words, the infant is, becomes, through the experience of the mother's being. Experience is implicit, below consciousness and yet, it is all that matters at this early stage of development. The infant becomes a full human being through these feelings of being and not before.

As mentioned earlier, by the *Third Critique,* and Whitehead all along, Kant and Whitehead do not presuppose a subject existing outside of, and prior to experience (as Descartes does); but nor do they dissolve the subject into the flux of experience (as Hume does). The subject is not self-perpetuating, but must be continually renewed. The subject does not outlive the feelings that animate it at any given moment. In this way, the ancient doctrine of Heraclitus that "no man ever steps in the same river twice, for it is not the same river and he is not the same man" is extended. Whitehead (1929, p. 29) says: "no thinker thinks twice and, to put the matter more generally, no subject experiences twice". Each new experience, including those which appear the same as previous ones – a repetition – is a fresh creation and a new subject. Novelty coexists with a sense of continuity that we actually feel from moment-to-moment.

This notion, as I pointed out earlier, has important implications for psychoanalytic work. There is always something repetitive in every transference relationship – relationships and forms of relating are being transferred from previous relationships into the therapeutic one, and yet it always includes some novelty. To start with, the transference relationship may be rigid on both sides: 'you are my mother' on the patient's mind, and 'you mean me' on the therapist side, but with the working through of the transference and its accompanying feelings, a symbolic 'as if' attitude begins to emerge, and with it, a transformation and a new transcendent transmission. If, for Freud (1920), the compulsion to repeat is more fundamental than the pleasure principle, for Whitehead, creativity – the new – is the universal of universals. There is a danger, however, with the notion of relentless novelty, for it can become meaningless repetition and, thus, static. If the process of being is based on process then process itself remains empty and repeatedly produces nothing but process; and therefore it never arrives at the genuinely new. Some patients suffer from stagnation and others from a rollercoaster of existence. Usually these states of mind alternate within the same individual, as evidenced in manic-depression. However, Whitehead is saying both, that there is nothing in an instant, for what matters is transition and process, and, also, that in concretion something becomes actualized. There is nothing in an instant and all we are is a series of instants. Whitehead explains the sense of continuity by inheritance. For the 'datum' of any new experience is largely composed of the remnants of immediately past experiences. But Whitehead's crucial point is that the subject as anything that exists in time, perishes. Locke's phrase that time is a 'perpetual perishing' runs like a leitmotiv through the pages of *Process and Reality* (Whitehead, 1929, p. 29, 147, 208). The fact that for Whitehead the subject is also a surperject, that is, not something that underlies experience, but something that emerges from experience, does not mean that Whitehead abolishes the subject. Indeed, for Whitehead (just as much as for Kant), there is nothing outside of experience, and no experience without a subject. Whitehead (Ibid., p. 166) states that "the whole universe consists of elements disclosed in the experiences of subjects". There is always a subject, though not necessarily a human one. Even a rock or an electron have experiences, and must be considered a subject–superject to a certain extent. Whitehead (Ibid., p.88), states that a falling rock "feels" or "perceives", the gravitational field of the earth. The rock is not conscious, of course; but it is affected by the earth, and this being affected is its experience. What makes a subject–superject is not consciousness, but unity, identity, closure and transcendence. In the moment of its actualization, a subject is entirely singular. Right afterwards, of course, the moment passes, and the subject is "objectified" as a "datum" for other occasions. The external world as datum feels the being before the mind can think. This is what Winnicott is describing in relationship to the infant and this is what Mrs. R did when she intuitively put something into action in relationship to her husband and myself, before she comprehended what she was doing, or what it meant.

For Whitehead, as for the psychotherapists, affect precedes cognition. It is only after the subject has constructed or synthesized itself out of its feelings, out of its encounters with the world, that it can go on to understand that world, or to change it. The primary function of theories is a lure for feeling; and one cannot do without such theories and such lures. Whitehead (1929, p. 184) goes as far as to say that philosophy should begin with a *"Critique of Pure Feeling"* instead of reason (which amounts to putting Kant's *Third Critique* first). Whitehead, like Plato exemplifies and encourages speculation, fabulation and invention, experiencing and attempting to rethink anew, so that one can stay ahead of himself.

These Whiteheadian and Platonic ideas and attitudes are most inspiring for psychoanalytic work. One may question: Are psychoanalytic theories a lure for feeling, or an attempt at explaining away? Does one take them to be cast in stone or fluid? Does one allow enough time and space for the feelings to emerge organically, so to speak, and endure them, without jumping into premature interpretations? Does one allow for one's interpretations to be precise enough and flexible enough? Are therapists 'hung up' on consciousness and making the unconscious conscious, in such a way that they miss the whole emotional experience in the process? Is feeling and emotion something that one feels, or something that one talks about and analyses? Does one have the 'courage', as Plato and Whitehead had, to acknowledge that one can only tell the most likely tale – in addition to understanding what great achievement this already entails? Does one allow oneself to speculate and confabulate enough, without fear of hallucinating? Does one allow oneself to hallucinate and enter the world of the unconscious as Jung did (with his dreams, manikins, stone, building of towers, drawing mandalas, etc.), without fear of going mad – or even when fearing going mad? Does one allow for the meaningless, as well as for the meaningful to emerge? Does one place more value on procedure and progress than on process? What does one mean by progress, anyway?

For Whitehead, becoming is the deepest dimension of being. Everything is an event; the world is made of events, and nothing but events: happenings rather than things, verbs rather than nouns, processes rather than substances. An event does not just mean 'X has happened to a subject'. Even a seemingly solid and permanent object is an event; or better, a multiplicity and a series of events – it is eventful at every moment, from second to second, even as it stands seemingly motionless, something is always happening. Heraclitus's river, like psychoanalytic sessions, never remains the same. At every instant, the mere standing-in-place of a pyramid is an event; a renewal, a novelty, a fresh creation, inasmuch as seemingly uneventful sessions are. What appears stuck is an event in motion, and what appears circular is a spiral. Whitehead (1929) says that, at the limit, an event may be just one particular occasion, a single incident of becoming, but more generally, it is a group of such incidents, a multiplicity of becomings – a nexus.

A nexus is "a particular fact of togetherness among actual entities" (Ibid., p. 20). When the elements of a nexus are united, not just by contiguity, but also by a "defining characteristic" that is common to all of them, and that they have all "inherited" from one another, or acquired by a common process, then Whitehead calls it a society (Ibid., p.34). Whitehead (1933, pp. 203–204) states that events and actual occasions are the ultimate components of reality, and that the real actual things that endure, including the pyramids and human beings (sometimes called "enduring objects") and which one encounters in everyday life experience, are all societies. One's Self-identity, or the manner in which one rallies to oneself, is the expression of the process by which one receives the past, reflects on it, and transforms it, again and again. For Whitehead, subjectivity is a process. What is basic is not the individual but the always ongoing, and never complete or definite, process of individuation, in Jung's terms. The therapist is immersed in-between what never changes and is forever changing in patients and in himself. Psychoanalytic sessions are archetypal and immanent, mythological and real. Man struggles to experience and understand the difference between become and becoming; between the fact that there is not continuity in becoming, and the fact that he is forever becoming. Man finds it difficult to grasp that becoming (gerund included) is not continual, because each occasion, each act of becoming is unique: a production of novelty, which is also a new form of "concrete togetherness" – something new has been added to the universe and, as in Plato's *Timaeus*, it marks a radical break with whatever was here before. This is what Bion (1975/1978) calls 'turbulence'; when everything is ongoing and changing, turbulence sometimes becomes sufficiently obtrusive to be given a name. Bion further speaks of Leonardo's obsession with drawing water and hair as a way of depicting the movement of the universe and of human nature. Order and disorder, permanence and flux are both necessary for the freshness of living. Psychoanalytic skill demands repetition, and imaginative zest is tinged with impulse. In Whitehead's words (1929, p. 338): "The act of progress is to preserve order amid change. Life refuses to be embalmed alive". And then, Whitehead (1938) speaks of the living emotion thus: "The energetic activity considered in physics is the emotional activity entertained in life" (p. 168); "All ultimate reason is in terms of aim and value. A dead nature aims at nothing. It is the essence of life that it exists for its own sake, as the intrinsic reaping of value" (p. 135); and that "existing is activity ever merging into the future" (p. 169).

In Plato's *Timaeus*, the living being is seen as eternity; psychoanalytic theories on child development follow along these lines. In psychoanalysis one needs both fluidity and firmness: a firm structured and theoretical framework which is yet capable of flexibility in action. Every session is a new session and every session has elements of repetition from previous seasons. As Whitehead said, every part of a man's history has been re-informed by the creative genius of his own present moment.

References

Bion, W. R. (1965). Transformations. *Seven Servants*. New York: Jason Aronson. 1977.

Bion, W. R. (1975–1978). *Four Discussions with W. R. Bion*. London: Clunie Press.

Bion, W. R. (1997). *Taming Wild Thought*. London: Karnac.

Freud, S. (1920). Beyond the pleasure principle. *Standard Edition*, vol. 18.

James, W. (1912). *Essays on Radical Empiricism*. Lincoln, NE: University of Nebraska Press, 1966.

Jung, C. G. (1957). Structure and dynamics of the psyche. *Collected Works*, 8. London: Routledge & Kegan Paul, 1970.

Jung, C. G. (2009). *The Red Book: Liber Novus*. Edited by S. Shamdasani. London: Philemon.

Kant, I. (1781). *First Critique of Pure Reason*. Translated by W. S. Phuhar. Indianapolis: Hackett Publishing, 1966.

Plato. (1965). *Timaeus and Critias*. Translated by D. Lee. London: Penguin.

Plato. (1979). *Complete Plato Works*. Edited by J. M. Cooper and D. S. Hutchinson. Indianapolis: Hackett Publishing.

Plato. (1997). Cratylus. *Complete Plato Works*. Edited by J. M. Cooper and D. S. Hutchinson. Indianapolis: Hackett Publishing.

Plato. (1997). Eponimis. *Complete Plato Works*. Edited by J. M. Cooper and D. S. Hutchinson. Indianapolis: Hackett Publishing.

Plato. (1997). Laws X. *Complete Plato Works*. Edited by J. M. Cooper and D. S. Hutchinson. Indianapolis: Hackett Publishing.

Plato. (1997). Letter VII. *Complete Plato Works*. Edited by J. M. Cooper and D. S. Hutchinson. Indianapolis: Hackett Publishing.

Plato. (1997). On Justice. *Complete Plato Works*. Edited by J. M. Cooper and D. S. Hutchinson. Indianapolis: Hackett Publishing.

Plato. (1997). Parmenides. *Complete Plato Works*. Edited by J. M. Cooper and D. S. Hutchinson. Indianapolis: Hackett Publishing.

Poincare, H. (1952). *Science and Method*. New York: Dover Publications.

Whitehead, A. N. (1925). *Science and the Modern World*. London: Free Association Books, 1925.

Whitehead, A. N. (1929). *Process and Reality*. Corrected ed., D. R. Griffin and D. W. Sherburne, Eds. New York: The Free Press, 1985.

Whitehead, A. N. (1933). *Adventure of Ideas*. New York: The Free Press, 1967.

Whitehead, A. N. (1938). *Modes of Thought*. New York: The Free Press, 1967.

Winnicott, D. W. (1971). *Playing and Reality*. London: Pelican Books, 1974.

Chapter 8

Being, Becoming and Modes of Being

Introduction

In this chapter, Heidegger is invited along with Whitehead into the consulting room. I have questioned the ground between metaphysics and psychoanalysis. Heidegger provides a complementary approach with a potential for awareness of psychological dimensions. His philosophy of Being provides both process thinking which mirrors contemporary psychoanalytic thinking, as well as a framework for it. If for the last 70 years Whitehead has been the philosopher of becoming, Heidegger has been the philosopher of Being. Heidegger, as Whitehead, is interested in finding new ways of thinking and of exercising the faculty of wonder. They both seek the dissolution of old certainties and the facing of new challenges.

In the context of this book, Heidegger contributes to the view of Being as process, as well as the concealment of Being as Absence. This is linked to Bion's views on transformations in 'O'.

Martin Heidegger on Being

Martin Heidegger (1977) is concerned with man as Being, with man as the openness to which and in which he presences himself and is known. For Heidegger man's life does indeed lie under a destiny sent from out of Being, but for him that destiny can itself call forth a Self-reorienting response of man that is real and is a true expression of human freedom. Similarly, Both for Whitehead and for psychoanalysts, man is conditioned by his past; for Freud, the early childhood traumas reverberate in the adult's personality and, Whitehead's theory of 'causal efficacy' illuminates the presence of the past in the present. Both also emphasize the

DOI: 10.4324/9781003261841-9

ultimate freedom of man, and of each 'actual entity', to choose, to select, to become other than what it was, to differentiate and unify. Neither for Heidegger nor for Whitehead nor for the psychoanalyst is there an ontological dichotomy between being and becoming – they are two indispensable aspects of existing.

For Heidegger, true thinking is never an activity performed in abstraction from reality. It is never man's ordering of abstractions simply in terms of logical connections. Genuine thinking is, rather, man's most essential manner of being human. Thinking is man's fundamental responding to whatever offers itself to him. Informed by recollection, it brings forth into awareness and efficacy whatever is presented to it now. Being manifests itself continually anew. In keeping with this, thinking can never be for Heidegger a closed system, rather it is a journey. Each thinker goes along in his own idiosyncratic way. Like Plato/Socrates in his dialogues, Heidegger is primarily a teacher. He does not want to guide others, nor to report what he has seen. He wishes the reader to accompany him on the way, to participate with him, and even to begin to build his own way through thinking, and not merely to hear about what it is or should be. Similarly, the psychoanalytic task involves participation, mutual cooperation and involvement with patients in their singular journey. There are two people alone together in the consulting room, creating the path they are walking on as they go along.

For the psychoanalysts, as for Whitehead, consciousness is only a later and ephemeral state of being, for layers of unconsciousness influence that tip of experience. Similarly for Heidegger, Being approaches and concerns the individual in whatever is, yet Being characteristically conceals itself as absence even in so doing. This absence manifests clinically as defence mechanisms such as blanking which evict the individual from his own being as he disowns aspects of himself. Hence thinking cannot readily find it out. The way through thinking to that place where man can open himself to the ruling of Being is difficult. It leads often through unfamiliar and even perilous territory. One is far from that open clearing. One is trapped and blinded by a mode of thought that insists on grasping reality through imposed conceptual structures. This is what Heidegger calls 'enframing', that is, an abstraction, a simplification or a reduction made in the service of some particular interest. Enframing encompasses both a necessity for potentially deeper and wider understanding as experiences are conceptualized, and the danger of reductionism when these abstractions are extended beyond their limits. This is what Whitehead (1929, p. 7) calls "the fallacy of misplaced concreteness". For Heidegger (1977), one cannot and will not come to that place where one can let what is, be. One does not perceive that the way by which true thinking proceeds can still prove to be the source of that unity which one strives after. This is the difference between becoming conscious and the coming to be of the Self, what Jung calls individuation. This also refers to what Bion calls transformations in K (knowledge) and transformations in O (Being).

In order to prepare the individual truly to think, Heidegger, in keeping with the tradition of speculative philosophy, often carries him beyond his facile conceiving to seek the ground of his thinking, but he does more, since, like Jung, he confronts the person repeatedly with the abyss – he strives to induce him to leap to new ground, to think in fresh ways. Hence, time and again, as we travel with him some precipice will confront us. One must often clamber through dark sayings and scale absurdities if one would follow these paths. This is a daunting prospect. Yet Heidegger has hope for those who go with him, for the ground he seeks to achieve belongs fundamentally to man as man. Hence he calls each person who reads him to come and find out. It is crucial that one experiences the turnings of these paths just where they happen. No element can properly be excerpted and considered in isolation, and none can properly be left out of account; for each element plays its part in the forward movement. For Heidegger as for Whitehead, it is always a matter of working out of the whole provided by the delimiting way pursued. In psychotherapy one works in and with limitations, one needs to build and be content to build finitely. However intricate the relationships to be expressed, however manifold the given meaning, it is important to set forth one facet at a time. One is trying to allow for both a tremendous rigour which makes great demands on the therapist and the capacity to let go in reverie, which makes equally great demands on him, if of a different nature. The therapist is in readiness to learn from the patient who is all the time teaching him and simultaneously, as Winnicott (1971) has pointed out, the therapist should know, theoretically, about the matters that concern the deepest or more central features of personality; otherwise he may fail to recognize and meet new demands on his understanding and technique when the patient is able to bring deeply buried matters into the context of the transference, thereby affording opportunity for mutative interpretation (by interpreting the therapist shows how much and how little of the patient's communication he is able to receive). If the therapist endures or perseveres, he may hope to experience the excitement of discovery as he finds himself intimately engaged in the pursuit of thinking and becoming, thereby approaching the essence of his being. According to the ancient doctrine, the essence of a thing is considered to be what the thing is.

Heraclitus's river in permanence and flux is at the very heart of psychoanalysis. Freud called it repetition and emergence, Bion called it turbulence, Jung, archetype incarnated and individuation, Winnicott, transitional object, Whitehead speaks of the past and the present creating the novelty of the future, and Heidegger of the unconcealment of Being.

Ms. T presented for therapy with a severe physical concern. She had spent most of her adult life with a debilitating neck and back pain. Over the years, she had sought a cure for her condition in many quarters, including physicians and less reputable modern-day gurus. She seemed to have taken in the latter fully and to follow their advice meticulously. A rigid system seemed to be established in her mind, a credulity in these questionable methods which had no bearings on her reality. From the start one could feel the competition she had placed between psychoanalysis and the 'feel-good' methods. As therapy progressed, one got the sense of being stone-walled with this person; there was an ongoing description of the multiple methods and rituals of her daily routine, the details and repetition of the experts words as mantra that needed to be continuously echoed for survival. The sessions became increasingly demanding; what she wanted from me was 'homework', rituals, exactitude, advise, anything which she could do by herself at home. The sessions felt draining and I could feel her disappointment and frustration. These feelings were named by me and almost immediately dismissed by her: "if only I could be more practical and give her tasks, therapy could take off for the better". The material to work with was barren; she said she remembered nothing from her childhood and dreams were absent. There was a sense that just being for the sake of Being was not an option for her, Being could only be either doing or blanking. Any interpretation to this effect met with rejection or else with a sense of enthusiasm to learn from me 'how to do being'. Suddenly, dreams began to appear in the consulting room. The patient felt astounded that she should dream in the first place, and of the nature of her dreams. These were filled with symbolism of an archaic nature, caves, prehistoric animals, underground tunnels, lost civilizations, and herself being transported from the entrails of the earth to a modern world of neon lights. I felt a sense of relief, a sense that her mind was compensating itself and that a one-sided ego attitude was being balanced in unconscious material. Being was approaching her, in Heidegger's terms. I felt the potential for something 'other' which could be closer to Being, and of her being in touch with a primeval being within her. Herself as a full being, androgynous and united, as opposed to a unidimensional fragmented Self. Something powerful was taking place inside her beyond her control and she felt disconcerted and disappointed, but never frightened, at least not outwardly, since as far as she was concerned these dreams had nothing to do with her. Associations would not come forth and blanking was resorted to. Another dream emerged which felt to her even more bizarre and nonsensical; in it she had become a hermaphrodite and was giving birth to a dead baby through her male's anus part. As she reported the dream, her mind went blank whilst mine was racing with imagery, but the potential of this dual being could not be realized, it could only give birth to itself and by itself as a stillborn baby, through her back passage, and through her male counterpart. Her dreams stopped altogether and she felt relieved that all that nonsense had stopped. I felt saddened, Being was not allowed to be and we were once again confronted with the absence of being, with still birth between us, and with the customary evacuatory and blanking defence mechanisms. Therapy was aborted soon after.

Bion's Views on Transformations and Invariance

In what follows I will be focusing more closely on Bion (1965), who following on similar lines, speaks of "transformation" and "invariance". Transformation means a change of form. In psychoanalysis one is constantly observing and performing transformations in oneself and in patients. Bion proposes the "O" sign for the original fact, the unknowable thing-in-itself in Kant's sense. One could say the O sign is both sign and symbol and is akin to Plato's receptacle, to the emergent container, to Jung's centre or matrix, and to Whitehead's percipient occasion, or experience as the thing-in-itself, and to Heidegger's Being.

If Freud and Klein had at their starting point the raw mass of instinctual impulses, Bion started from a reality which is unknown because unknowable, which he named "O". Psychoanalysis became the expression of O.

Bion distinguishes different groups of transformations in the mental area including knowing about O and transformations in O. Knowing about O includes rigid motion transformations, projective transformations and transformations in hallucinosis, while transformation in O contrasts with these three in that it is related to change, growth, insight and becoming O. According to Bion, reality cannot be known by definition, but it can be 'been' – he calls this becoming O. Reality has to be 'been'. The events of the session are the O of the analyst's transformations – the patient's associations, his behaviour, gestures, all that happens in the session is O for the analyst. O is always related to some aspect of physical or psychic reality (ultimate, unknowable reality, absolute truth, the thing-in-itself, the infinite, the unknown). Psychotherapy is concerned with the reality of the patient's personality in such a way that one goes beyond 'knowing about it', even though this knowing (K link) is an important part of the analytic process. Transformation in O is 'being what one is', and in this being what one is, or process of becoming, or individuating process, always has a disruptive character. This is what Bion calls 'the catastrophic change' which is both feared and resisted, as well as desired.

For Bion, the analytic task is to grasp the transformations from O, in order to interpret them, in the hope of inducing the transformation K to O in the patient. Psychoanalytic interpretations are the results of a series of transformations which stem from a certain original experience between analyst and patient, and which reveal the invariance of that experience, but in order to carry out this task one must tolerate the suffering and frustration associated with 'not-knowing' and 'not-understanding'. One must be able to forget and to eschew desire and understanding and to let some space for his intuition to emerge, for the psychic reality he is trying to comprehend in the patient is not originally an object of the senses. One must have patience and wait for the selected fact (Poincaré, 1952), which could give coherence and meaning to the unknown, newly evolving O. The psychoanalytic experience implies both a knowledge about oneself and being oneself. Becoming O implies assuming responsibility for one's own feelings whatever their nature (responsibility for murderous feelings, feelings of 'madness', incestuous feelings, etc.). When transformations in K threatens appearance of transformations in O, the fear of psychological turbulence, of catastrophic change arises. At those times the fluidity of Heraclitus river is transformed into dangerous 'rapids', so to speak. A resistance to change from K to O takes place out of fear associated with insight. More than that, it is the terror of recognizing oneself beyond recognition. The therapist needs to allow himself to move away from the tranquil Heraclitus's river into the 'rapids', together with the patient. He has a little dingy, call it the fact that he himself has been psychoanalysed, but the 'rapids' are tumultuous, fast and fierce and the patient's conscious and unconscious attacks in the therapist's use of it, that is, in his capacity to think psychoanalytically, can jeopardize the efficiency and freedom that at other times he can more safely provide. At such times, the therapist's intuition is called for with a special urgency and a particular state of mind which Bion calls faith. This allows him to approach the psychic reality that cannot be known but can 'be been'.

This act of faith – faith in the psychoanalytic process – is a scientific act of faith quite different from religious meaning in that it has an unconscious and unknown event as its background. Faith, act of faith and mystery refer to a mental activity which operates in a non-sensuous dimension (in the sense that it lacks form, colour, smell; it is not accessible to the senses), even though it can sometimes be expressed in terms derived from the language of the senses. Faith is what is not; it refers to intuition and to faith in the process based on intuition. The therapist can only think and speak from his own heart and mind and address his mind and that of the patient to an analysis of experience. Whitehead (Price, 1956) seems to have said that it is a well-founded historical generalization, that the last thing to be discovered in any science is what the science is really about.

Interpretation facilitates the process of exploration and progressively approximates to the O of the session, that is, the psychoanalytic object, which psychoanalysis is said to be about. The analytic endeavour is a lure for feeling, that is, to build up understanding to the point at which an interpretation will emotionally move the patient. The analytic experience, the coming together of two personalities, cannot be known in its essence but only in its manifestations in the two people involved – analyst and patient. Each of these experiences in its own way is representative. This is the first transformation, and then transforms it in and for communication to others. It is then possible for the two versions of the same situation, that is, the transformation of the patient and that of the analyst, to be compared with each other. As mentioned earlier, for Bion the preconception is given to, and searches for, a particular experience with which it can match and then be complete. In Winnicott's terms the breast, mother, is found and created because it was always there – in the infant. This mating renders it emotionally real and is associated with the subjective experience of realizing something, that is, understanding its meaning: a conception is born. Having become a conception, a new preconception is ready to mate. This whole process is that of thoughts growing in complexity and depth.

The analyst must search the material for invariants in order to understand the shifts. For Bion, these are to be found in the pre- and post-catastrophic stages. These are found in the domain represented by the theories of projective identification, internal and external objects; for example, to demonstrate that certain apparently external emotionally charged events are in fact the same affects as those which appeared in the pre-catastrophic event. According to Bion, in the pre-catastrophic stage, the analysis is unemotional, theoretical and devoid of any marked outward change. Hypochondriacal symptoms are prominent. The material lends itself to interpretations based on Kleinian theories of projective identification and internal and external objects. Violence is confined to phenomena experienced by psychoanalytic insight; it is, as it were, theoretical violence. By contrast, in the post-catastrophic stage the violence is potent, emotion is obvious and aroused in the analyst. Hypochondriacal elements are less obtrusive. In the pre-catastrophic stage the analyst may hear of pains and aches of different natures, complaints about relatives or friends, that is, of elements which appear external and due to firm instances but which are, in essence, hypochondriacal pains and other evidences of internal objects in a guise appropriate to their new status as external objects. These are then the invariants or the objects in which invariance is to be detected. In listening to the invariance; the relating to it and the changes to it, the analyst gathers the flux in the mind. He tries to help the patient transform that part of an emotional experience of which he is unconscious into an emotional experience of which he is conscious. The transformation is transcendent, that is to say, it goes beyond transforming that part of an unconscious emotional experience into a conscious one, for it extends to the emotional state evoked in the individual and it also gives durability to the power to evoke emotion.

The interpretations that effect the transition from knowing about O to becoming O are those establishing complementarity. That is, the interpretation should be such that the transition from knowing about reality to becoming real is furthered. The therapist needs to know what kind of action is required to effect the transformation from K (knowledge, insight) to 'becoming' or 'being'. Knowing about growth is not the same as growth in becoming. Accretions of knowledge further K, but not O, that is, it increases knowledge, but does not produce O. It is not the same to have learnt psychoanalytic theories and to be psychoanalysed.

Interpretations are important in order to further transformations from K to O, from a Bionian perspective. However, there are many occasions when interpretations are not even needed, for experience itself is its own interpretation. After all, what takes place in the consulting room is an emotional situation which is itself the intersection of an evolving O with another evolving O: in so far as the analyst – and patient alike – becomes O, he is able to know the events that are evolutions of O. The only way of knowing psychic reality is through intuiting it and of knowing O by becoming. The analyst is concerned to comprehend the life of the mind itself, the living mind from the mind's own life. Causal connections do not tell him about life itself.

Although it sounds plausible to say that the events of the psychoanalytic experience are transformed and formulated, and that their value therapeutically is greater if they are conducive to transformations in O, and less so if conducive to transformations in K, it could be argued that engaging emotionally, dialectically and psychologically is itself transforming. One could also add that transforming involves making bearable, as opposed to a gigantic transformation in the patient's personality. In other words, being at one with O, being O, is different from a projective identification in which one becomes God, for this is madness, megalomania, as opposed to real. One could also argue against the dichotomy between interpretations and transformations, in the sense that interpretations themselves are transformations. Whatever one's views, one thing seems to be true for all: man would much rather know himself than be himself, especially those aspects retrieved by analysis from obscurity.

Mrs. U, a therapist herself, presented for psychotherapy. She has undergone a lengthy analysis in the past, but needed to be in further analysis as a requirement for further training. A year into the therapy, she spoke about the difficulties she was experiencing with one of her own patients. She describes him as callous, devious, sadistic and selfish, and describes how he leaves her feeling in a state of emotional exhaustion and with physical symptoms, including severe stomach aches. The power of a negative transference is often discussed and the counter-transference feelings experienced by her – the therapist. Mrs. U seems to understand theoretically the underlying psychological mechanisms operating between her and her patient, but prefers to "keep them in mind" as opposed to addressing them. Her opinion is that "mentalization" is a superior method to psychoanalysis and might work better with certain patients with severe psychopathology. She often jokes about her own sadistic impulses and how many years it took for her to come to terms with this aspect of herself. This, of course, she discovered in her previous analysis and not in the present one with me and thus, she feels there is no need to talk about it anymore. My sense is that she is in 'rivalry' with O, and with me, as opposed to being O. Her composed demeanour is characterized by envy, hate, love, megalomania and 'acting out', as opposed to acting and experiencing. For some time, I have been making transference interpretations between us which seem to parallel her patient's behaviour with her. This has always been dismissed outright. In fact, she says that "she does not believe in the negative transference", but instead thinks that addressing it with the patient is a way "of building a case against the patient, Kleinian style". In a particular session I pointed out that she seems to fear any challenge or confrontation both with her patient and with myself, and even more so with herself. I then asked what she feared might happen "if we left psychoanalytic understanding aside and were to be open to the feelings in the room". She responded defensively by saying that she did not think there were any negative feelings towards her patient or me. However, she returned for her following session to inform me that "we could no longer work together since we had very different styles and because I had crossed the line". When asked in what way she felt this was so, she replied that my implication was that she was as envious, attacking, destructive and vile as her patient. I said that she sounded upset and angry with me and that perhaps we could think together as to what might be happening between us. She denied there were any difficult feelings between us that needed discussion and with that session she terminated her analysis. As she walked out, I felt rather unwell both physically and mentally – stomach ache, tiredness, puzzled, frightened, shocked, guilty. I wondered if I had underestimated my patient's psychopathology. She phoned a couple of days later to resume her sessions. I agreed, for I felt that at last we could work through the negative transference which had been lurking for so long. Instead, Mrs. U stated that she was not prepared to work through her rage again with me, for, as she told me at the beginning, she had already done so in her previous therapy. She said this as a matter of fact, as if emotions, including rage, were static and motionless, and one could work through them once and for all. I said that it sounded as if it terrified her moving from a position of "knowing about her rage to being it"; and from being the therapist with her patient to being the patient with me. This was followed by a brief moment of silence but then, she composed herself and ended the therapy – this time for good.

Another patient complained, in his habitual manner, about the lack of effect the psychoanalytic sessions have on him. He asked: "How is it possible that I have been coming to analysis for so long (more than a decade twice a week) but nothing has changed in my life? I continue to have low self-esteem and lack of confidence in myself. I loathe myself". Through my own countertransference feelings I felt this was said with provocative rage and with the purpose of maintaining the status quo of sadomasochism. I said: "It might well be that you have not got anything from the analysis, but I also wonder if you would rather remain oblivious to the changes which have in fact occurred". He responded angrily and denied that there had been any changes in him at all. In a soft, non-retaliatory voice I said: "You came to therapy because you felt numb and completely disconnected from your own feelings and thus, alienated from yourself and from others, now your complaint is that you feel too much". My comment released shock and rage and this was the moment when my patient became real to himself. We worked through his anger and frustration in relationship to his analysis and to me, to the world at large, and most importantly towards himself and his "strict and emotionally dead parents", for many months to come. Slowly and gradually something shifted, making our encounters more trustworthy and safe, if also more tumultuous. Our sessions frequently involved sheer frustration and despair, mixed with sadness and gratitude. I would not say that having to endure and work through these feelings is an easy task; it is challenging and taxing for both of us. However, inasmuch as it is difficult, it also feels genuine and true. The raw emotions are in the open and neither of us is hiding away from the experience.

Matte Blanco's Levels of Emotion and Modes of Being

There are several levels of increased emotion that psychoanalytic procedure enables. Matte Blanco (1975) speaks of unconscious sets with progressively deeper sets embracing several of the sets at more superficial levels. For Blanco, there are two modes of Being in humans, what he calls the bi-logic dynamic, which is composed of both symmetrical and asymmetrical logic. The former is composed of the unconscious (repressed and unrepressed), that is, of emotion and dream logic. This is based on Freud's model of the unconscious and its five characteristics, namely, condensation, displacement, absence of negation, timelessness and confusion of inner phantasy and outer reality. In Blanco's model, the deepest level of increased emotional state is where all affects are interchangeable. This represents the ultimate reality, Bion's O, Heidegger's unconcealment of Being, and the emergent container of infinite potentiality. Asymmetrical logic, on the other hand, relates to consciousness, to bivalent thinking and Aristotelian logic. The five strata of mental life (distinguished by the nature of symmetry and asymmetry appended in each), or the level of increased emotional states are as follows:

1   Common sense logic (Aristotelian), factual assertions.
2   Simile.
3   Metaphor and symbol.
4   Paradox and contradiction.
5   Silence of the mystical contemplation. Organizing principle: propositional function: all affects are interchangeable.

The fifth level represents the container, the matrix, the ultimate reality, or a vast reservoir of infinite possibilities, of thoughts awaiting thinking, from which everything else emerges. All change is a component of O, and O is both static and in flux. Life itself propels man towards fluidity and change and, simultaneously, there seems to exist a fundamental mind, a primordial mind, or an archetypal mind which seems to remain unaltered in every man. One wonders if O has been called O because it symbolizes the Omega for everything – the alpha and the omega: its beginning and its end. The Greek letter omega seems appropriate as a linguistic symbol and as a cultural one, for in one's divagations one constantly returns to one's Greek forefathers and their dialectic method.

Reality as the Process of Becoming

For Winnicott (1971) the 'transitional object' refers to symbolism in time. In other words, it refers to becoming and describes the infant's journey from subjective to objective. The transitional object is what one experiences as process into experience. Instead of being tempted to focus on the opposite terms – what is static – or even in the space between the objects, Green (1983) draws attention to the idea of the journey. The journey expresses the dynamic quality of the experience, implying a move in the space linked with time. The transitional space is not just 'in between'; it is a space where the further subject is in transit, taking possession of a created object in the vicinity of a real external one, before he has reached it. The transitional space is a process, and thus, not surprisingly, Winnicott titled one of his seminal works: *Playing and Reality*, in a similar way to Whitehead who called his *Process and Reality*. They both seem to be saying that there is no distinction between playing and reality and process and reality, that is, playing is reality and process is reality, and reality is a process of becoming.

References

Bion, W. R. (1965). Transformations. *Seven Servants*. New York: Jason Aronson, 1977.
Blanco, M. I. (1975). *The Unconscious as infinite Sets. An Essay in Bi-logic*. London: Karnac.

Green, A. (1983). *The Dead Mother.* Edited by K. Mollon. London: Taylor & Francis e-Library, 2005.

Heidegger, M. (1977). *The Question Concerning Technology and Other Essays.* London: Garland Publishing.

Poincaré, H. (1952). *Science and Method.* New York: Dover Publications.

Price, L. (1956). *Dialogues of Alfred North Whitehead.* New York: Mentor Books.

Whitehead, A. N. (1929). *Process and Reality.* Corrected ed., D. R. Griffin and D. W. Sherburne, Eds. New York: The Free Press, 1985.

Winnicott, D. W. (1971). *Playing and Reality.* London: Pelican Books, 1974.

Chapter 9

Quaternio

Introduction

In attempting to introduce the notion of quaternio I am aware of the difficulty of speaking of something which is so complete in itself. What I mean by this is that the quaternio is a stable element of the emergent container and in this sense it is not dynamic since it is a full square, circle or mandala. From this angle quaternio is not becoming but become: a primordial image of man and the soul. Yet, quaternio also represents a goal, an aim, a process, a becoming. Thus, the quaternio could be conceptualized as a being that is forever becoming, and a being that always is. The quaternio encompasses absence, suffering, conflict, creativity, novelty and future. In other words, the quaternio represents the process of creation and the striving of man towards completion.

The Quaternio in Plato's *Timaeus*

In Chapter 1 Plato's *Timaeus* (1965) took centre stage to introduce the concept of the receptacle – the emergent container. Here, *Timaeus* is brought forth anew because there is another important aspect in those opening sentences of Plato's *Timaeus* regarding the quaternio, the number four: "one, two, three – but where, my dear Timaeus, is the fourth ...?" Timaeus will later on in his presentation explain how the Universe and human beings in it came about. They were born out of the four essential elements: fire, water, air and earth. In *The Republic*, Plato (1997) discusses the four cardinal virtues: wisdom, temperance, courage and justice. Similarly, for the alchemists, and certainly for psychoanalytic work, as well, the work demands not only intellectual

DOI: 10.4324/9781003261841-10

and technical ability, but also a moral attitude. In other words, psycho-analytic work is a psychological and moral or ethical undertaking.

The Quaternio in Jung's Alchemical Notions

Jung (1946, p. 143) quotes John Grover's (1330–1408) *Confessio Amantis* saying: "*bellica pax, vulnus dulce, suave mallum*" (a warring peace, a sweet wound, a mild evil). Into these words, the old alchemist put the quintessence of his experience. They contain all that the ego can reasonably demand of the opus, and illuminate the paradoxical darkness of human life. Submission to the fundamental contrariety of human nature amounts to an acceptance of the fact that the psyche is at cross purposes with itself. Alchemy teaches that the tension is four-fold – forming a cross, as a form of suffering expresses psychic reality, and carrying the cross is therefore an apt symbol for the wholeness, and also for the passion which the alchemist sought in his work.

An exclusively rational analysis and interpretation of alchemy – and of unconscious contents projected into it – must necessarily stop short at the above parallels and antitheses, for in a total opposition there is no third – *terbium non datur*.

Whitehead (1925), in agreement with Jung and the alchemists, is of the opinion that science comes to a stop at the frontiers of logic, but nature does not – she thrives on ground as yet untrodden by theory. *Venerabilis* nature does not halt at the opposites; she uses them to create, out of opposition, a new birth.

In Plato's *Philebus* (1997), Socrates says:

> See what I mean by the third: I treat all the offspring of the two as a unity, a coming into being created through the measures imposed by the limit. The craftsman must be the fourth. And whatever is said to be, consists of one and many, having in its nature limit and unlimitedness.

Similarly, in his writings, Jung speaks of the quaternio, about the recalcitrant fourth, about completion, about mandala, about whole-ness, about the four functions of the psyche: thinking, feeling, intuition and sensation. For Jung, the quaternio is one of the most important archetypes and has also proved to be one of the most useful schemata for representing the arrangement of the functions by which the conscious mind takes its bearings. It is like the crossed threads in the telescope of human understanding. The four functions of the mind are as important for consciousness and for providing a person's compass of the world, as they are in the negative. That is to say, it is crucial to grasp which function is less developed, or more unconscious within each person, and what one can do about it.

The cross formed by the points of the quaternity is no less universal and has in addition the highest possible moral and religious significance for Western man. Similarly, the circle, as the symbol of completeness and perfect being, is a widespread expression for heaven, sun and God; it also expresses the primordial image of man and the soul.

The quaternio as the two – conscious and unconscious, patient and therapist, finite and infinite, personal and archetypal – plus the third, which is that which the analytic couple creates: the new, and the fourth: the receptacle, that is, the emergence of the three, or what makes the third possible. The three become one and add one to the three. The quaternio as the uniqueness of every analysis.

There is both in Plato and in Jung a deep intuition of how a new world, and the inner world of human beings, came to be. The universe, human beings, were all born out of absence; and man's psyche, his soul, is forever aiming at bringing the four together towards completion, towards transcendent function. This is enabled by the Jungian transference of kinship libido, where two human beings, patient and therapist alike, seek each other and become involved at the deepest level of the soul. Here a marriage of opposites and a marriage of two minds is cultivated and enabled, thereby giving birth to something so creative that it transcends both. "In being ourselves, we are more than ourselves", says Whitehead (1925, p. 23).

This is enabled by kinship libido which encompasses both Freud's sexual libido, biologically rooted, and Jung's psychic libido, creating thereby a third, made possible by the receptacle – the fourth. The quaternio represents a goal, an aim, a process, a becoming. It is an urge towards ideal perfection with all the imperfections that entails. A being that is forever becoming, and a being that always is.

Jung (1951) expounds that the recognition of the anima gives rise, in a man, to a triad, one- third of which is transcendent: the masculine subject, the opposite feminine subject and the transcending anima. With a woman the situation is reversed; the recognition of the animus gives rise in a woman to a triad, one-third of which is transcendent: the feminine subject, the opposing masculine subject and the transcending animus.

The missing fourth element that would make the triad a quaternity is, in man, the archetype of the wise old man, and in woman the Chthonic Mother. These four constitute a half-immanent and half-transcendent quaternity – an archetype which Jung (1946) had called 'the marriage Quaternio'. The marriage quaternio provides a schema for the Self, and for the structure of primitive society.

Perhaps one can think of Plato/Socrates as an archetype, as the wise old man bringing himself forth for the cure and enlightenment, the nurse of all becoming and change. And of Diotima, in Plato's *Symposium* (1997), as a representation of a similar figure in the feminine.

Jung (1946, p. 45), speaks of how the structure of the Mercurial Fountain reveals the *tetramenia* – fourfold nature – of the transforming process, already known to the Greeks. It begins with the four separate elements, the state of chaos, and ascends by degrees to the three manifestations of Mercurius in the inorganic, organic and spiritual worlds; and, after obtaining the form of Sol and Luna – the precious metals of gold and silver, but also the radiance of the gods who can overcome the strife of the elements by love – it culminates in the one and invisible – incorruptible, ethereal, eternal – nature of the anima, the *quinta essentia, aqua permanens,* tincture, or *Lapis Philosophorum*. This progression from the number 4 to 3 to 1 is the 'axiom of Maria', which runs in various forms through the whole of alchemy as a leitmotif. The initial state of wholeness is marked by four mutually antagonistic tendencies – 4, the circle, 3, a masculine number, and out of it comes the feminine number, 2 (the interpretation of uneven numbers as masculine, and of even numbers as feminine is general in alchemy, and originated in antiquity). Male and female inevitably constellate the idea of sexual union as the means of producing the 1, which is then consistently called the *filius regius or filius philosophorum*. The child is a symbol of the Self, and the quaternio is a symbolic expression of this.

Jung speaks of the potential intrinsic values of the individual, and how they can only be realized through relationship – with oneself and with others – by transcending the collective attitudes and responses and by developing one's unique capacities: by 'individuating'. In Whitehead's (1929) terms, by magnifying the individual actualities and promoting strength of experience – "the many become one, and are increased by one" (p. 21). In Plato's terminology, it is the absence, the sickness and the suffering that is the receptacle, the nurse of all becoming and change. As mentioned earlier, a receptacle that contains the container and the contained, thereby enabling the emergent container to emerge.

For Whitehead (1929), it is impossible for experience to exist independently: experience arises out of that which is lived. Every drop of experience is a novel weaving of the world of preceding experiences out of which that drop arises. The many experiences constituting the world of the past are brought together into a new experience. Whitehead (Ibid., p. 21), states: "it lies in the nature of things that the many enter into complex unity" – the many become one. But there are many experiences arising in each new moment, so each 'one' is also a part of the 'many'. "The many become one, and are increased by one". This is what Whitehead calls 'concrescence' – the process in which the universe as many things acquires an individual unity in a determinate relegation of each item of the 'many' to its subordination in the constitution of the 'novel' one. The novel one is the 'satisfaction', that is, it is the culmination of concrescence into a completely determinate matter of fact. Man's soul – mind or psyche – is the current cumulative flow of his experience. Jung (1963) adopted the expression '*unus mundus*' – one world – from the alchemist Gerhardus Dorn to designate the transcendental postulate of the unity underlying the multiplicity of the empirical world.

Arthur Schopenhauer defined space and time as the *principium individuationis*, noting that he had borrowed the expression from Scholasticism. The *principium individuationis* was the possibility of multiplicity – the world as will and representation. The term was used by Eduard Hartmann, who saw its origin in the unconscious. It designated the 'uniqueness' of each individual set against the 'all-one-unconscious'. Jung (1912) wrote that diversity arises from individuation, and that this fact validates an essential part of Schopenhauer's and Hartmann's philosophy in profound psychological terms. I would add that Whitehead's metaphysics validate Jung's notion of individuation. Whitehead's process theory is about becoming. In other words, it is concerned with relatedness, differentiation, unification, identity and novelty, and with how each new creation augurs future ones, "the many become one, and are increased by one" (Whitehead, 1929, p. 21). In a series of papers and presentations later, in 1916, Jung developed his concept of individuation. Jung's (1921) concept of individuation is crucial to his thinking and to our psychology. As for Whitehead, it refers to an ongoing process of becoming the individual as distinct from the general. Individuation is a process of differentiation.

For centuries, philosophy has taught that there are four causes: the *causa materialis* – the material, the matter out of which, for example, a silver chalice is made. The *causa formalis* – the form, the shape into which the material enters. The *causa finalis* – the end. The *causa efficiens*, which brings about the effect.

Martin Heidegger (1977) questions this quaternio: "why are there just four causes?". He argues that for a long time man has been accustomed to representing cause as that which brings something about. In this connection, he says, to bring about means to obtain results, effects. The *causa efficiens*, but one among four causes, sets the standard for all causality. However, in this quaternio, the four causes are the ways, all belonging at once to each other, of being responsible for something else. Similarly in the *Symposium*, Plato (1997) speaks of the craftsman bringing forward or producing, generating, begetting, uttering or eliciting. That is, Plato speaks of the four causes being at play within bringing forth.

Along similar lines, Poincaré (1952) describes the process of creation of a mathematical formulation. For him, a new result or the creation of a novel entity emerges when known elements which had remained scattered and seemingly alien to each other are united. This is the process of disorder into order or the advance from disjunction to conjunction in Whiteheadian terms. This enables us to see each of these elements in relation to the whole. The new fact has value for, and by, itself, and it alone gives a value to the old fact it unites. The world is too complex to comprehend but if we can introduce some order into this complexity, it may become available to us.

Therapists need to deal with fragments before meaning emerges – what Bion, inspired by Poincaré called 'the selected fact'. This is another way of saying that the many become one, and are increased by one. This is at the heart of empathy and kinship libido, where everything in the world and, through relationship – dialogue with oneself and with others – becomes one. This is also Jung's concept of individuation, containment, connection, and transcendent function; Bion's (1963) alpha–function and container–contained, pre-conception meeting realization and thereby creating conception; Whitehead's (1929) concrescence; Winnicott's (1971) moment in which the breast – mother – is both found and created simultaneously, and Plato's receptacle.

The geometrical figures of Plato: the Forms, as he calls them, in understanding the formation of the Universe and of human beings, are also present in psychoanalytic and analytic insight. If Freud was to concentrate on the triangle and the triangular relationships of the Oedipus Complex, Jung was to add another angle, so to speak, in being more attuned to Plato's intuition regarding the quaternio.

The Changeless and the Four elements in (Human) Nature

After Critias's presentation of the Atlantis, Timaeus asked: "What is that which always is and had no becoming, and what is that which becomes but never is?" Here, Plato, Timaeus and the psychotherapists, are grappling with the essential nature of their own existence. One is dealing with the river of Heraclitus – the river into which one cannot step twice, for its waters are in constant flux, and yet, a river which is always a river. The river of the 50 minutes of a session with a patient where the therapist dips in and out. Sometimes he dips only the tips of his toes. At times he allows himself to go for a full swim, or even dive in – often nearly drowning. The possibilities are endless, including the possibility of not getting wet, at all.

On the one hand, there is the intelligent nature of the universe, of the psyche, of the soul which is changeless and invisible; and, within it, the fire, the air, the water and the earth. That is, a secondary understanding of all these things belonging to what moves, is moved by others, and which sets others in motion. Two causes for man's being – one constant, the other in constant motion, made possible by the third, the receptacle, the nurse of all becoming and change. Some patients are stuck, have been incarcerated in their emotional world for years, resist suffering, and defend themselves with all their might. There is a vicious cycle of repetition that always seems to be present, and yet, every session is a different session, every minute, every moment is a new beginning.

References

Bion, W. R. (1963). Elements of psycho-analysis. *Seven Servants*. New York: Jason Aronson, 1977.
Bollas, C. (1987). *The Shadow of the Object*. London: Free Association Books.
Green, A. (1983). *The Dead Mother*. Edited by K. Mollon. London: Taylor & Francis e-Library, 2005.
Heidegger, M. (1977). *The Question Concerning Technology and Other Essays*. London: Garland Publishing.
Jung, C. G. (1912). Transformations of symbols of libido. *Collected Works*, vol. 8.
Jung, C. G. (1916). The structure of the unconscious. *Collected Works*, vol. 7.
Jung, C. G. (1921). Psychological types. *Collected Works*, vol. 6.
Jung, C. G. (1946). *The Psychology of the Transference*. Translated by R. F. C. Hull. London: Routledge, 1983.
Jung, C. G. (1951). Aion: Phenomenology of the self. The ego, the shadow, the syzygy: Anima/Animus. *Collected Works*, vol. 9.
Jung, C. G. (1963). *Memories, Dreams, Reflections*. Edited by A. Jaffe. London: Fontana Press, 1995.
Plato. (1965). *Timaeus and Critias*. Translated by D. Lee. London: Penguin.
Plato. (1997). *Plato Complete Works*. Edited by J. M. Cooper and D. S. Hutchinson. Indianapolis: Hackett Publishing.
Plato. (1997). *Philebus. Plato Complete Works*. Edited by J. M. Cooper and D. S. Hutchinson. Indianapolis: Hackett Publishing.
Plato. (1997). *Republic. Plato Complete Works*. Edited by J. M. Cooper and D. S. Hutchinson. Indianapolis: Hackett Publishing.
Plato. (1997). *Symposium. Plato Complete Works*. Edited by J. M. Cooper and D. S. Hutchinson. Indianapolis: Hackett Publishing.
Poincaré, H. (1952). *Science and Method*. New York: Dover Publications.
Whitehead, A. N. (1925). *Science and the Modern World*. London: Free Association Books, 1985.
Whitehead, A. N. (1929). *Process and Reality*. Corrected ed., D. R. Griffin and D. W. Sherburne, Eds. New York: The Free Press, 1985.
Winnicott, D. W. (1971). *Playing and Reality*. London: Pelican Books, 1974.

Chapter 10

Formlessness

Introduction

Absence as both formlessness and empty space is considered in Chapter 10 in relation to emergent container which is the matrix of all things, but is itself formless, to Jung's archetypes and to mutual unconsciousness. They are also likened to Winnicott's therapeutic procedure, which is to afford opportunity for formless experience, and for creative impulses which are the stuff of playing, and to Whitehead's (1929, p. 105) ideas for whom "Spontaneity arises from empty space, and life itself is a characteristic of empty space". Psychoanalysis rests on the premise that at the heart of human nature lies a formless something, a Self, a mystery, and it seeks both to solve and to preserve this mystery.

Jung's Use of Symbols

Timaeus says that, although fundamental, the receptacle is a difficult and vague notion. It is nature which receives all bodies, but itself is devoid of all forms, or any characteristics it is to receive from elsewhere. It is the matrix of all things, but is itself formless. It is an absence, an invisible void, and yet, it is all creative. The receptacle is nature, it is matrix, it is absence, but the 'It' is not an 'It' at all: language is necessary and it gets in the way of what one wants to express. In other words, in talking about the receptacle, one is talking about what is not, and it is precisely in this form of being, which is a 'not-being' that everything becomes possible.

Given these characteristics, the receptacle could be understood as archetype, by which the personal life of the individual will both fill in

DOI: 10.4324/9781003261841-11

the details of the empty space and will be filled by it. Jung's archetypes are formless, empty concepts in themselves. Archetype is a concept empty of specific content. Archetype in analysis involves the Self as pure potential and emptiness at the centre. The whole course of individuation is dialectical, and the so-called 'end' is the confrontation of the ego with the 'emptiness' of the centre (*Letters of C. G. Jung*, 1951–1961). In other words, individuation is dialogue with emptiness. There is always danger of filling the space with 'knowing', distorting countertransference. For Jung, the emotionally infused image is the primary organizer, or the most fundamental coherent unit of the human psyche. The receptacle can be considered a myth that becomes reality in the living experience of this particular individual, at this particular time, in this particular relationship; and a reality that becomes myth. The receptacle as archetype is a container for all that is possible in a human life; for all experiences a human being can have. It is also a communication between what always is and what is forever becoming, between what is permanent and what is fluid. Receptacle could be said to be the only real thing in the universe, and it is formless.

The process of containment is the making of future: emergent containment. This intuitive concept meets the needs of symbol formation in analysis. Analysis both creates and contains its evolution, that is, it is an emergent container. Man contains his own container. He needs an open and formless container alive in all its modalities: Platonic receptacle, archetypal container, psychological container, for to try to pin it down to either of its categories, or attempting to fill it in with detail, kills the concept and the potential of the experience – foreclosing, closing down, a far reaching and far richer concept. "Every location involves an aspect of itself in every other location" (Whitehead, 1925, p. 114). This applies both to container and contained and to these different notions of container: internal/external.

Jung uses symbols, thereby allowing the formless emergent container to emerge. Some have argued that Jung's container is impersonal and makes use of the collective language of alchemical mythology, compared with the more personal, interactional and down to earth, model of Bion's container–contained. The consequence is that because of the alchemical allegory Jung's container model may appear to become too concrete, that is, not formless. This is a danger for any model because it becomes correspondingly unwieldy. There might be an element of truth in this criticism of Jung's container model, for alchemical allegory or archetypal imagery can become both endowed with endless possibilities, but also conservative in the particular evocation. However, the opposite argument is also a valid one, in that it is through allegory and metaphor, without pinning it down, that the significance of container is not concretized. One could argue that the mythical is real and personal and that the personal is just anecdotal.

It has been argued that because Jung's Tavistock model inherently fails to integrate the emotional experience of the potentially threatening aspect of container–contained, the psychoanalytic material reported by Jung in *The Tavistock Lectures* (1935) contains "undigested facts", elements which correspond to the beta-elements described by Bion. One could argue that this criticism of Jung is unsubstantiated, in the sense that Jung's model is interactional: two people in the alchemical bath together, and in that Jung clearly recognizes the dangers of his model threatening the psychoanalyst. This is described vividly in the example of the psychiatric nurse who took on the patient's psychosis (and in Jung himself with his own patients). The aspect of container–contained, with all the dangers and perils that it entails for both participants, is for Jung a condition for psychic growth and this view is implicitly and explicitly developed throughout Jung's writings. One could also argue that there is a fallacy of misplaced concreteness regarding the so-called 'digested facts and undigested facts', since facts continue to evolve, they continue to be chewed over, and this is something which Jung demonstrates through his life's work, experiences and writings. What could be a fair criticism of Jung is that, although he recognizes the psychic infection and transformations that psychoanalytic procedure brings about for both participants – the alchemical transformation in the vas – this transformation, however, is explored by Jung mainly in its positive aspects. For instance, although the process may be arduous, the outcome is welcoming and growth promoting. Bion (1965), on the other hand, is emphasizing different forms of transformation; one positive, the other detrimental. The former relates to transformations in O (being) and transformations in K (knowledge), the latter to transformations in hallucinosis.

Both Jung and Bion, in their own ways, were in touch with the psychotic core of the personality, both within themselves and with their patients. Jung, in particular, went to the depths of his being in his encounter with the unconscious where he met the elderly Elijah and blind Salome. Much before that, right from the beginning of his life, that is, from a very early age, Jung was grappling with his dreams, visions, existential struggles, mysteries and imagination – his phallus dream, his stone, his manikin, his towers, his mandalas.

Formlessness and Emptiness as Experience of Being

I am attempting to describe the indescribable and finding ways of talking about pure potential and undefinable dynamism. Formlessness and emptiness are viewed as a recurrent experience of being which can only be realized as representation. Bollas's (1987) concept of the 'transformational object' might be relevant here. A transformational object is experientially identified by the infant with processes that alter self experience. It is an identification that emerges from symbiotic relating, where the first object is 'known' not so much by putting it into an object representation, but as a recurrent experience of being – a more existential as opposed to representational knowing. Not yet fully identified as an Other, the mother is experienced as a process of transformation, and this feature of early existence lives on in certain forms of object-seeking in adult life, when the object is sought for its function as a signifier of transformation. Thus, the quest in adult life, is not to possess the object; rather the object is pursued in order to use it as a medium that alters the Self, where the subject as-supplicant now feels himself to be the recipient of enviro-somatic caring, identified with metamorphoses of the Self.

The memory of this early object relation manifests itself in the person's search for an object (a person, place, event, ideology, etc.) that promises to transform the Self. Aesthetic moments do not sponsor memories of a specific event or relationship, but evoke a psychosomatic sense of fusion that is the subject's recollection of the transformational object. Christopher Bollas says that, although the emphasis here is on the positive aesthetic experience, it is well to remember that a person may seek a negative aesthetic experience, for such an occasion points to his early ego experiences and registers the structure of the unthought known. The 'unthought known' represents those experiences in some way known to the individual, but which the individual is unable to think. It stands for those early schemata for interpreting the object world that preconsciously determine the person's subsequent life expectations. In this sense, the unthought known refers to preverbal, unschematized early experience/trauma that may determine one's behaviour unconsciously, barred to conscious thought. Some patients repeat traumatic situations because through these they remember their origins existentially. In adult life, therefore, to seek the transformational object is to recollect an early object experience, to remember not cognitively but existentially – through intense affective experience – a relationship which was identified with cumulative transformational experiences of the Self. Its intensity as an object relation is not due to the fact that this is an object of desire, but the object being identified with such metamorphoses of being. In the aesthetic moment, the subject briefly experiences, through ego fusion with the aesthetic object, a sense of subjective attitude towards the transformational object, although such experiences are re-enacted memories, not re-creations. The search for symbolic equivalents to the transformational object, and the experience with which it is identified, continues in adult life. Balint (1968) speaks of a search to repair the 'basic fault'. The term basic fault refers to the structural deficiency in the personality of subjects who during the early stages of development formed certain types of object relations – which later became compulsions – in order to cope with a considerable initial lack of adjustment between their psychological needs and the care provided by a 'faulty' environment devoid of understanding. The effects of the basic fault on a person's character structure and psychological dispositions predispose the person to certain illnesses.

It should not be surprising that varied psychopathologies emerge from the failure, as Winnicott put it, to be disillusioned from this early and significant relationship. That is to say, from the failure to allow oneself to be disillusioned and work through this mourning process of development. Many patients will invite the analyst into a pathological transformational relation, for example, to create confusion in order to compel the analyst to misunderstand them. This is a negative transformation and may represent the transfer of a pathological mother–child relation, but even here the analyst may be experienced as a generative transformational object. One of the mother's transformative functions must be to frustrate the infant. Likewise, aesthetic moments are not always beautiful or wonderful occasions – many are ugly and terrifying but nonetheless profoundly moving because of the essential memory tapped.

It is in the apparent calm of the consulting room that one faces the evolution and emergence of the most primitive parts of the mind, and what is not, what is formless, provides the matrix, or the receptacle from which phenomena appear. What is not can be called absence, receptacle (Plato), archetype, container (Jung), or proto-mental phenomenon (Bion), basic fault (Balint), or the unthought known (Bollas). The important thing is that it transcends experience, for the proto-mental state, or the state of mutual unconsciousness can be characterized as neither psychic nor physical. It is its evolution, rather, which produces psychic or physical phenomena, prior to that, it is a system in which these aspects remain undifferentiated, formless.

Formless Concepts in Psychoanalysis

For both Freud and Jung, the dominance or breakthrough of deep unconscious processes was associated not only with madness but also with creativity: the creativity of the unconscious. Both were fascinated by madness or even idealized it, but, of course, not all afflicted persons appreciate or benefit from their psychosis. Some are permanently broken with no sign of breakthrough, but only breakdown. Others may not even realize they are ill, but drift dully at a low level of existence that barely approaches human. Many people carry their illness as a stranger, or a burden they do not really feel is part of themselves; it is an alien that alienates them. The intensity and all-consuming quality of psychotic experience seems to have passed them by; it has never taken on meaning, except as a curse. Indeed, it can be a blessing or a curse.

For Bion, too, the unprocessed and unthought data: the beta-elements are a characteristic of the primitive matrix from which thoughts develop, and alpha-elements are the primitive elements of thought derived from the basic data of the mind by the process of alpha-function. Both beta and alpha-elements and beta and alpha-function are hypothetical entities, constructs, formless concepts; they are both myths. Bion (1965), says that the term alpha-function is, intentionally, devoid of meaning. For him, it is a mythical apparatus which could perform the function of processing emotional experiences (which may occur in either waking or sleeping states). Beta-elements are also an empty concept in that it is a name for whatever-it-is that appears in the mind when alpha-function fails to operate, that is, when it cannot generate 'dream thoughts' which can be stored as memory or used for thinking.

Bion's concept of the proto-mental apparatus is also an equally formless/empty concept, which, in theory, includes functions of the mind in emotions, and bodily states which are not as yet distinguished from each other. Furthermore, Bion defines O as the void and formless infinite from which is 'won' the object that is known. Further still, Bion took the importance of the oscillation between the paranoid–schizoid and the depressive position move as a crucial one for mental life for a different reason than Klein; for Bion it represented the basic mechanism of thinking. It describes the move from the state of formless chaos to that of coherence which suddenly develops through the operation of the selected fact (Poincaré, 1952).

Freud (1920) posits two 'empty concepts': the Life and Death instincts. Klein (1946) does the same on *Some Notes on Schizoid Mechanisms* regarding the concepts of splitting and projective identification.

Formless Experience

Winnicott (1971), states that the person one is trying to help knows a new experience in a specialized setting. The experience is one of a non-purposive state, a sort of ticking over of the unintegrated personality. Winnicott refers to this as formless: non-purposive being, as opposed to purposive activity. For Winnicott, therapeutic procedure is to afford opportunity for formless experience, and for creative impulses, motor and sensory, which are the stuff of playing – and on the basis of playing is built the whole of man's experiential existence. Whitehead (1929, p. 105) states that "spontaneity arises from empty space" and "life itself is a characteristic of empty space and not space occupied". It is difficult to imagine that things can get any more formless than this.

Consciousness is the pinnacle of all the unconscious processes that have already entered the actual occasion. As Whitehead (1929, p. 161) puts it: "consciousness is the feeling of negation. Negative perception – absence, what 'is not' – is the triumph of consciousness". Most of what psychotherapists do is based on mental activity which operates in a non-sensuous dimension. In other words, it lacks form (and colours and smells etc.), and it is an act of faith, in that it has a formless, unconscious and unknown event as background. What they do is to try to give form to the formless and to let formlessness form them: that paradoxical. Empty space and formlessness is the emergent container of all potentialities, including the culmination of consciousness. It is as if the whole universe of psychotherapy emerges from formless black holes of anti-matter. Psychologically speaking, there are two black holes in the room – patient and therapist – or two unconscious minds, uniting, expanding and creating a third. Most of the psychoanalytic work takes place at the level of unconscious communication between two people, or unconscious communicating to unconscious, and then ... something happens between, within and beyond the psychoanalytic couple. Formlessness and empty space – reverie – are the vehicle of interconnections in the psychoanalytic couple. One needs both to allow for empty space and to create space for psychological development.

Most psychoanalytic concepts are formless concepts, they are myths. The term 'myth' includes not only typical social myths such as the Oedipus, but also a person's representation of an event. For example, the analyst's description of a session, or the psychoanalytic myth itself – the myth of two giving birth to a third – the wounded healer which embodies absence, becoming and the receptacle, etc. At the heart of human nature lies a formless something, a Self, a mystery of which all conceptualizations are inadequate representations. One does what one can. Plato, Whitehead, Jung, Bion, Winnicott and Freud all tried to solve this mystery and to preserve it.

References

Balint, E. (1968). *The Basic Fault*. London: Tavistock Publications, 1969.
Bion, W. R. (1965). Transformations. *Seven Servants*. New York: Jason Aronson, 1977.
Bollas, C. (1987). *The Shadow of the Object*. London: Free Association Books.
Freud, S. (1920). Beyond the pleasure principle. *Standard Edition*, vol. 18.
Jung, C. G. (1935). The Tavistock Lectures. *Collected Works*, vol. 18.
Jung, C. G. (1951–1961). Letters of C. G. Jung, vol. 2. Edited by G. Adler and A. Jaffe. London: Routledge, 1976.

Klein, M. (1946). Notes on some schizoid mechanisms. *Envy and Gratitude and Other Works 1946–1963*. London: The Hogarth Press and the Institute of Psychoanalysis, 1975.

Plato. (1965). *Timaeus and Critias*. Translated by D. Lee. London: Penguin.

Poincaré, H. (1952). *Science and Method*. New York: Dover Publications.

Whitehead, A. N. (1925). *Science and the Modern World*. London: Free Association Books, 1985.

Whitehead, A. N. (1929). *Process and Reality*. Corrected ed., D. R. Griffin and D. W. Sherburne, Eds. New York: The Free Press, 1985.

Winnicott, D. W. (1971). *Playing and Reality*. London: Pelican Books, 1974.

Chapter 11

Interrelations

Introduction

Following Whitehead's theory of prehension, interrelations are considered to be intrinsic to human nature. By prehension Whitehead means feeling, and the experiential process of becoming involves the reception, response and transmission of feelings. Man is inherently empathic.

Whitehead's Views on Interrelations

Psychotherapy is a lure for feeling. Feeling is relational. Relations are precognitive and affective. For Whitehead (1929, p. 312) "Relations are fundamental". Each thing arises out of its social relations and is internally constituted by these social relations. Whitehead uses the term 'prehension' for the fact by which one actual occasion takes up and responds to another. Sense perception is one sort of perception, but it is far from being the only one, for the person's life is filled with experiences of 'non-sensory' perception, including his awareness of the immediate past, to the feelings he has of the 'withness with the body'. Interrelations are always present in man's existence. This is what Whitehead calls "causal efficacy", that is, "the sense of derivation from immediate past, and of passage to an immediate future" (Ibid., p. 178). Such an immediate past "is gone and yet is here. It is our indubitable Self, the foundation of our present existence" (Whitehead, 1933, p. 181). Even though the 'thing-in-itself' is unknowable or unrecognizable, nevertheless it affects the person, in a particular way. The affective connections are intrinsic to the very core of any experience in space and time. For Whitehead, there is no need to impose the categories of understanding from above, in order to give these

DOI: 10.4324/9781003261841-12

impressions form, or to yoke them together. As he put it, "in such a process of feeling, causality does not need to be established extrinsically, since the datum includes its own interconnections" (Whitehead, 1929, p. 113).

For Whitehead, all experience is emotional, whether conscious or unconscious and "feelings" are identical with "positive prehensions" in general, which are all the ways in which entities interact with one another, or affect one another (Ibid., p. 220). To be more precise, Whitehead distinguishes between "physical prehensions", in which an actual entity feels, or interacts with other actual entities, and "conceptual prehensions", in which an actual entity feels, or interacts with "eternal objects" – potentials including qualities and concepts. Most prehensions are "hybrids" of both these kinds, but in every case, a prehension is a process whereby an actual entity feels something. To feel something is to be affected by something. In Whitehead's account, every prehension consists of three factors: the "subject" which is prehending, namely the actual entity in which that prehension is a concrete element; the "datum" which is prehended; the "subjective form" which is how that subject prehends the datum (Ibid., p. 23). Elsewhere, in another list of the same three factors, Whitehead (1933, p. 176) defines subjective form as "the affective tone determining the effectiveness of that prehension in that occasion of experience". (Note that Kant's transcendental aesthetics provides the basis for one of Whitehead's most important notions, that of "subjective form".)

There are also "negative prehensions" in which an actual entity excludes other entities or eternal objects from being felt, or from any such interaction. However, Whitehead (1929, p. 220) says that these "can be treated in their subordination to the positive prehensions" and

"Each negative prehension has its own subjective form, however trivial and faint. It adds to the emotional complex, though not to the objective nature" (Ibid., p. 41).

Feeling is relational and "essentially a transition" (Ibid., p. 221). Feeling always points from place to place; and feeling inherits from past and projects towards the future. Through the process of feeling, different points in space are united in the solidarity of one common world (Ibid., p. 72), and every process of feeling produces time: both as "perpetual perishing" of the entity that feels, and as "the origination of the present in conformity with the 'power' of the past" (Ibid., p. 210). This "power" of the past, which marks time as transition, and which forces relations from one point in space to another is the force of "repetition". Every "present" moment forcibly "inherits", and thereby repeats, what came before. "The notion of 'simple location' is a fallacy, because it is inconsistent with any admission of repetition, or of a time that intrinsically refers to another time" (Ibid., p.137). To establish a particular space–time location is always, first of all, to affirm repetition, and thereby establish a difference by referring elsewhere and else when, to other stretches of space and other periods of time. Time is transition, and repetition produces newness of difference.

These Whiteheadian notions can be seen as the epitome of the interrelations of all things, including a crucial paradox to be maintained and not dissolved in psychoanalytic practice and thinking. For example, Winnicott (1971), reminds the therapist of the importance of sustaining the paradox that the infant both creates and finds the breast (mother). What is being addressed here is another crucial paradox to be respected in psychoanalytic work: this involves the fact that the 'repetition compulsion' which Freud identified in patients – feelings, behaviours, thoughts, actions, transference, stalemate, sameness, which keep recurring with a particular insistence – is simultaneously also the mark of difference and motion. As with Winnicott's paradox, unless the therapist is open-minded to this paradox and perceives the nuances of repetition, and how repetition is also evidence of difference as much as stalemate, the therapist will get stuck in attempting to explain/ understand the patient's present difficulties exclusively by reference to the past, as if an exact replica of past feelings had been transported to the relationship with the therapist, when, in fact, actual entities are not primarily located in space and ordered by time – rather, spatial location and temporal sequence are generated through the becoming of these actual entities. That is to say, an entity composes or creates itself by feeling the other entities that have influenced and informed it; and it feels them as being spatially and temporality distinct from itself. This self-distinguishing action of each new entity, and the consequent differentiation of time and space, is a necessary concomitant of the very process of feeling, of every "pulse of emotion" (Whitehead, 1929, p. 163). There is both a fresh creation of space–time and an immediate perishing, or 'objectification'. The "emotional continuity of past and present ... is a basic element from which springs self-creation of each temporal occasion ... How the past perishes is how the future becomes" (Whitehead, 1933, p. 238). Every analysis is a new analysis, every session is a new session, every patient is a new patient. Only when a process of feeling has completed itself and perished can it be circumscribed as a datum to be felt "a definite fact with a date" (Ibid., p. 230). Under these conditions, every feeling is a "vector feeling", that is to say, feeling from a beyond which is determinate and pointing to a beyond which is to be determined (Whitehead, 1929, p. 163).

Even mechanistic (and quantum-mechanistic) interactions are feelings, according to Whitehead; and even the most "simple physical feeling" is at once both "an act of perception" and "act of causation" (Ibid., p. 236). The "emotional feeling" with which the individual receives sensa like colour is not fundamentally different in kind from the manner in which subatomic particles relate to one another; it is only much broader in scope (Ibid., p. 163). Feeling, as such, is the primordial form of all relation and communication, and psychotherapy is, above all, a lure for feeling. Feeling can therefore be conceived as a vector of transmission, as reference and as repetition. These three dimensions are closely intertwined. Every feeling involves a reference to another feeling, but reference moves along the line of the vector. The feeling entity is "conditioned" by, or is an "affect" of, all the other entities that it feels (Ibid., p. 236), and the entity, in turn, becomes a condition, or a cause, for whatever subsequent entities feel in their own ways. Every entity thus "conforms to the data", every entity also selects among, shapes and alters these data, until it reaches a final determination. In so doing, it offers itself to be felt by other entities in its own turn, so that it is "referent beyond itself" (Ibid., p. 72). The "objectification" of the entity, once it has been completely determined, allows for its repetition, and this repetition is the key to the future as well as to the past; for every new process of becoming "involves repetition transformed into novel immediacy" (Ibid., p. 137).

This is where the importance of grasping the transference–countertransference in psychoanalytic work resides. That is, in keeping the paradox referred to earlier – repetition- encompassed newness – for this way one may understand the transference as transferential repetition for novel immediacy, which includes both the personal and the archetypal dimensions of it. This paradox is also implicit in Winnicott's view that 'we need to fail our patients in order to succeed'. That is, the therapist needs to fail patients in the same way they were failed in earlier relationships, especially in relationship to mother, since in the repetition of the general and the specific failure, novelty is enclosed.

An act of feeling is an encounter – a contingent event, an opening to the outside – rather than an intrinsic, predetermined relationship – and feeling changes whatever it encounters, even in the act of 'conforming' to it. For Whitehead, as for the psychotherapist, everything is connected to everything else, events are entirely interdependent, yet also mutually independent. The world, and the world of emotions, are both a disjunctive multiplicity of discreet entities, and a continuous web of interconnections. Neither of these connections can be ignored: "the many become one, and are increased by one" (Whitehead, 1929, p. 21). The therapist needs to find connections and meaning in the patients' narrative and experience and, simultaneously, to allow for the unconnected and meaningless.

Whitehead's and Deleuze's Views on Interrelations

Similarly, for Deleuze (Deleuze and Guattari, 1987), things are irrevocably connected to one another, despite not having any sort of underlying element in common. He provides an account of the receptacle, as well as of Jung's synchronicity when he speaks of the independence between flowers and insects. This idea of everything being interconnected even when having nothing to do with each other, poses fundamental questions for psychoanalytic understanding. For instance, does the therapist receive the projective identification from the patient and get affected by it because he has a similar pathology (or similar unconscious, unanalysed aspects), where the patient can lodge his, or merely because his human/ common archetypal and existential humanity will find a hook? Does the therapist lend himself emotionally and intellectually with a willingness and porosity to receive whatever the patient needs to communicate? In other words, does the therapist share a common pathology with patients in actual terms? Do they share a common archetypal potential pathology within them and this is enough for the exchange and the impact? Or does the therapist have nothing in common in a particular aspect, like the wasp and the orchid and yet the projection feeds the projective identification and vice versa? Is this pure empathy? Kinship libido? And/or all of the above?

Interconnections and Independence

No entity can be completely isolated, because it is always involved in multiple relations of one sort or another, and these relations affect the entity, cause it to change, but this is not to say that the entity is determined by these relations, for the entity has an existence apart from these particular relations, and apart from other 'terms' of the relation, precisely insofar as it is something that is able to affect, and to be affected by, other entities. The entity is a function not just of its present relations, but of the whole history of relations, in which it has affected other entities and has been affected by them. Whitehead (1929) says that from the quantum level up, each "actual occasion", or process of becoming, both embodies interconnection, and asserts its own independence for all the past occasions from which it is derived and to which it is connected. It both inherits everything that comes before it and breaks away from everything that it inherits. Each "novel entity" is at once the togetherness of the "many" which it finds, and also it is one among the disjunctive many which it leaves; it is a novel entity, disjunctively among the many entities which it synthesizes. The many become one, and are increased by one. In their natures, entities are "many" in process of passage into conjunctive "unity" (Ibid., p. 21). Conjunction and disjunction, unification and diversification, must always go together, in the "process of passage" which is "the ultimate metaphysical truth". Whitehead's concrescence is the "production of novel togetherness" (Ibid., p. 21).

Synthesis precedes cognition, and it alone renders cognitive judgement possible. In itself, the act of synthesis is primordial, pre-logical and pre-cognitive. Synthesis is an action "produced by the imagination, which is a blind but indispensable function of the soul without which we would have no recognition whatsoever, but of which we are conscious only very rarely" (Kant, 1781/1966, p. 30).

Whitehead (1938, p. 136) states that "the notion of empty space" is "the vehicle of spatial interconnections". Any local agitation shakes the whole of the universe. The distant effects are minute, but they are there (here). The spatial universe is a field of force, or a field of incessant activity.

The analytic experience is the coming together of two personalities, and it is also a process of binding by which something is "won from the void and formless infinite" (Milton quoted in Bion, 1965, p. 162). Transformations take place at the level of experience (O), and at the level of insight (K knowledge). The sense of inside and outside, internal and external objects, container and contained are all associated with K. Kinship is both bringing together, and knowledge which brings together. In that sense kinship is knowledge and knowledge is kinship. In other words, not only does one 'individuate' – becomes himself through relationship, that is, through kinship libido with oneself and with other (s)/another – but also knowledge itself is about bringing together, into a unity, two or more elements: thoughts, ideas, images, feelings, etc.

Psychoanalysis is the investigation of relationships through a relationship and it attempts to open both partners to the emergent experience. An emotional experience cannot be conceived of in isolation from a relationship. Alpha-function installs empathy. Emotion flows between container and contained binding them together. Thus conjoined or permeated or both they change in a manner usually described as growth. Mother and infant are, to start with, a unit, and so are patient and therapist. A pre-conception meets realization and creates a conception. Mating involves kinship and relationship. Transference and countertransference are inseparable from each other. Everything has to be interrelated for even when one cannot find the connection, at all times, something unknown is doing something, one does not know what, to the universe. Whitehead's (1929, p. 21) chosen phrase to speak of this interconnection of all things is: "the many become one, and are increased by one". Man's conscious and unconscious being is always in close relationship, although its threads of connection may at times be invisible. Man's waking and dreaming life are also closely interconnected. Projection and projective identification go hand in hand, as well. The mechanism of projective identification enables the infant (adult and patient) to connect, or to deal with primitive emotion, and so contributes to the development of thoughts. The interplay between the paranoid–schizoid position and the depressive position is also related to the development of thoughts and thinking. Symbol formation is a dialectic between the paranoid and the depressive position.

Through experience the therapist knows that the psychoanalytic process, the event, is specific to the two participants (patient and therapist) involved at that particular time. Whitehead (1938, p. 97), states: "Process and individuality require each other". In separation the meaning evaporates. The form of process – the appetition – derives its character from the individuals involved, and the characters of the individuals can only be understood in terms of the process in which they are implicated. Thus, as Bion says, the therapist needs a new theory for every patient. A difficult problem arises: how can the notion of any generality of meaning be justified? If the process depends on the individuals, then, with different individuals the form of process differs. The same difficulty applies to the notion of the identity of an individual conceived as involved in different processes. The point is that everything is interrelated and that every individual thing infects any process in which it is involved. In therapy the observer infects the observed and vice versa. This is Jung's notion of *coniunctio* and contagion. In one sense there are two individuals in one room, but in another they both are part of a unity with different reflecting mirrors, yet one can also make generalizations and abstractions: "the differences arising from diversities are not absolute. Analogies survive amid diversity" (Whitehead, 1938, p. 98).

The immediacy of the psychoanalytic endeavour is the realization of the possibilities of the past, and is the storehouse for the potentialities of the future. Meaning itself is a conjunction of relationship and feeling. At times, patients' attention is directed to finding evidence of meaning, but not finding what the meaning is. Linking interpretations have little effect then in producing change until the patient sees that he is tapping a source of reassurance to provide an antidote to his problem and not a relational solution to it.

Anti-relating and Intersubjectivity

For Winnicott (1969), object relating denotes a relationship where the object is not perceived at all as having any existence independent of the subject's identificatory omnipotence, but it is entirely disposable by that subject; on the other hand, 'the use of an object' implies that the object is seen as an entity independent of the subject, but object usage pre-supposes object relating. For Jung too, object relating – the relation-ship between mother/infant or patient/therapist is the basis for individuation: the container for it.

Perhaps a crucial consideration is the extent of the projective identifica-tory processes and whether they are in the service of binding the object into inseparability, and thus, the extent to which that (unconscious) motivation is claustral – anti-thoughts, anti-reality, anti-function, anti-mind – or whe-ther it is used in order to interconnect. All the psychological defence mechanisms that the therapist observes in the psychoanalytic sessions with patients – repression, regression, denial, disavowal, attacks on linking, excessive projective identification, dissociation, etc. – refer in one way or another to anti-relating and anti-interrelations with oneself and with others. Winnicott (1949) identified a precocious split of the mind from body as the precursor of the 'False Self'. He posited that trauma may have been the experience of disruptions to the state of 'going on being' in early infancy.

All defence mechanisms are anti-relational in one respect and, in another, they are relational, for they are forms of communication intrinsic to human nature. One might question if the psychoanalytic method may be attracting people to analysis as a therapy that shares a phobia of the body and an identification and an exaltation of the mind. In other words, the therapist must be aware of his own inter-relations and anti-relations, or splits.

Both for Lambert (1981) and for Freud (1900), there seems to be a paradoxical and enduring problem of the human condition which appears to have a tendency to resist the very experience it longs for – patient's request and resist the therapist's help. The problem is com-pounded by the fact that the resistance is affirming something very useful, namely, the protection of the Self for Lambert and that of the ego for Freud. If for Freud we are perpetually involved in a dynamic dance between transference on the part of patients or in counter-transference on the part of therapists, for Lambert, we are also involved in resistance and counter-resistance. The therapist may resist the patient's personality as a whole or aspects of it, especially those aspects which have remained unresolved within himself.

If the experience of mutual interaction and involvement that goes on between analyst and patient is the goal of analysis, the interpretation is merely the means by which this goal is provided. If the aim of interpretation is to make possible an experience of the *coniunctio*, the coming together of patient and analyst is an intersubjective whole of mutual relatedness. This shifts the model of the analytic container from the analyst's mind, as Bion thinks of it, to the analytic relationship itself, the analytic vas as Jung calls it, in which containment occurs via the relationship, the emotional struggle and the to-ing and fro-ing that takes place between patient and analyst. The emotional struggle is the container, as well as that which is contained. It is the fermentation of this intersubjectivity that allows for the emergent container. The concept of the container exemplifies both the interrelations that it entails, but also the movement, that is, the fluidity of the container concept itself from being viewed as a state of mind, to taking place within relationship, to being the emotional struggle itself – understanding reached out of difficulty is containment.

Human Beings as Social Animals

For good or for ill, human beings are all interrelated since they are group animals: social animals. The person's individual psychic make-up is intimately related to others, both the tendency to form constructive working groups and the potential or valency as Bion calls it, to forming any of the basic assumptions. The group is essential to the fulfilment of a man's mental life (Bion, 1963). The group as a unit operates whether its individual members intend to, or are aware of it, based on basic assumptions which are shaped by the intense emotions of primitive origin. Basic assumptions express a shared unconscious phantasy of an omnipotent or magic type as to how to achieve its goals and satisfy its desires. All basic assumptions are emotional states that tend to avoid the frustration implied in learning from experience, and even more so in learning from pre-experience, when learning implies effort, pain and contact with reality. Bion identified three main categories of basic assumptions:

Basic assumptions of independence
Fight/flight
Pairing.

In basic assumption of independence the group holds the assumption that it is meeting so that somebody on whom the group depends absolutely should satisfy all needs and desires. The collective belief is that there is an external object whose function is to provide security for the group as an 'immature organism'. In other words, credence is given to a protective deity whose goodness, potency, and wisdom are not questioned.

The basic assumption of fight/flight consists in the group's conviction that there is an enemy who must be attacked or avoided. In other words, the bad object is external and the only defensive activity vis-à-vis this object is its destruction – fight – or avoidance – flight.

The basic assumption of pairing involves the collective and unconscious belief that, whatever the present problems and needs of the group, something in the future or somebody still unborn will solve it. In other words, that there exists a messianic hope. Hope is often put in a couple whose unborn child will be the saviour. In this emotional state what matters is the idea of the future, rather than the solution of the present problems.

When speaking of basic assumptions, it is important to remember that this primitive emotional level that manifests itself in every group coexists with another level of functioning that is the one belonging to the work-group. The work-group requires from its members cooperation and effort. It is a mental state that implies contact with reality, tolerance of frustrations and control of emotions. The task, which can be painful, but which is carried out rationally, promotes the growth and maturity in the group and its members – it is opened to learning, to new insights, new experiences and fresh conflicts.

Similarly, John Donne (1624) had an understanding that his Self, his being, was not separate from that of others, but is part of a common substrate: 'involved in mankind'. Similarly, Bion's (1975/1978) notion of a primordial mind which seems to remain unaltered in every human being and Jung's notion of the collective unconscious formed by archetypes runs along these lines, as well. Human beings seem to be interconnected by inborn and typical patterns of behaviour, like a treasure house of accumulated life experiences (which the individual may not have necessarily experienced in his lifetime, but which his common ancestors have). In other words, what links the whole of mankind is emotion – emotion as libido and as archetype.

Plato's Receptacle as the Epitome for Interrelations and Potentialities

Breuer recognized the importance of reclaiming the repressed elements in the mind from the unconscious; reclaiming thereby order from chaos. Freud then understood this reclamation took place in the setting and through interpretation of the transference relationship. Klein greatly elaborated the significance of internal objects and in so doing described the inner world of object relations. Bion took a greater step in abstraction when he recognized that underlying all of this was what he termed the psychoanalytic object O; representations of which could be described in the session, by meaning evolving out of a relationship. However, Whitehead, Winnicott and Jung took it to a further level still in that, for them, the relationship itself is the meaning. According to Whitehead (1933, p. 134), "The Receptacle, as discussed in the *Timaeus*, is the way in which Plato conceived the many experiences of the physical world as components in each other's natures". It is Plato's doctrine of the medium of interconnection and intercommunication of all things. "The receptacle imposes a common relationship on all that happens, but does not impose what that relationship shall be" (Ibid., p. 150). It is what allows for process with retention and connectedness and which embodies all possibilities. It is what enables "the many becoming one, and being increased by one". It is a process that transcends itself.

This process is at the heart of psychoanalytic work. The universe of one's potentialities is the receptacle of which one partakes. The therapist has an opportunity to become the container contained by the receptacle, enabling patients to be contained, in a constant motion of being, becoming and transmitting, in a constant motion amid the changeless, which enables the past to be present in the present, and urges towards future potentialities. The Freudian transference, 'the percipient occasion' (as Whitehead calls the actual experience) and the Jungian transcending future coming together in an event between the therapist and the patient. The receptacle receives all occasions of therapist and patient in communion, and all experiences of the world and transcends them. It is what can make possible a compound of reception, anticipation and transformation. It is the guiding principle of the universe and of every man. It is what allows for the living emotion. Whitehead (1929, p. 231) states: "In my personal feeling at any moment there are more than the objects before me, and no perception of objects will exhaust the sense of a living emotion". Plato too implicitly refuses to abstract the 'living emotion' from the bare intellectual perception. "The percipient occasion is its own standard of actuality", says Whitehead (1929, p. 145), which can be understood to mean that the experience, in this case the experience shared between therapist and patient, is its own evidence – it is its own illumination, the real thing, the thing in itself. Man cannot get away from emotion; perception is always clothed with emotion and the percipient occasion is always an event as process, the flowing movement. An emotion, an experience, or the percipient occasion may appear as a moment in time, but it is not; it has a history, it becomes, it perishes and it transforms all at once – it is a process.

Frames, frames of reference, analytic and psychoanalytic theories and thinking, abstractions, systematization, observation, description are important in psychoanalytic work, but most importantly and simultaneously, the therapist needs dream-like reverie and, above all, to allow himself to feel the full impact of the experience with the patient, whatever that may be. He needs system, but most importantly, he needs living understanding, and whether one likes it or not, the essence of the creative advance involves absence, decay, transition, loss, displacement, suffering, fear, confusion. It is out of man's psychotic core that at times the most sublime in him is born. If the therapist's quest is to understand and to understand understanding, he needs to be aware that understanding is never a completed static state of mind: it always bears the character of a process of penetration, incomplete and partial. There is often an understanding beyond his area of comprehension. In Plato's words: "We can only tell the most likely tale". In Plato's *Timaeus*, the understanding of the universe requires that one conceives in their proper relations to each other the role of the receptacle, absence, archetype, the container, causation, self-creation, contemporary independence and transcendent function. In psychoanalytic work, these relations, in addition to the relationship between patient and after therapist are necessary for the understanding of human nature. An important function of the therapist as a container involves the recognition of what is going on, which includes recognizing the dangers, the shadows, of what is happening and offering the possibility of containing it for the patient, so that it does not threaten with annihilation. The therapist can be helpful both as a container for the feelings which are already present, and as an emergent container for the emergence of patients' feelings and emotions. He deals with human needs and with the human need to be understood. Through kinship libido, through empathy, through relationship, the therapist attempts to overcome the demon of absence and sickness by taking it over by contagion, enabling thereby a new world of possibilities, potentialities, creativity and imagination. The Platonic tradition itself is the receptacle, the emergent container of this process for the therapist. Plato was speculating about the collective unconscious of his time, and it is still evolving two and a half thousand years later through the thinking of Freud, Jung, Klein, Bion, Winnicott, Whitehead, Meltzer, Green, Fairbain, Balint, etc. Individually and collectively they have developed Plato's intuitions and ideas of their own. Like Plato, and of course Socrates, the psychoanalytic forefathers represent the world they inherited and the one they created; the one the present day therapist has inherited and is presently creating. He is in the making.

The Notion of 'Not-Been-Born' and the 'Imaginary Twin'

At the Tavistock Lectures of 1935, Jung had spoken about the dreams of a ten-year-old girl and had commented that she had not been born entirely. This had an impact on Beckett (1977–1979) for whom "birth was the death of him" (1976). Not only Jung's Tavistock Lectures, which both Bion and Beckett attended, but also Bion's analysis of Beckett had a profound and continuous impact on them both. Their work runs in parallel, both with regard to certain themes and to certain forms of presenting those themes. Beckett struggled constantly in his literary work with meaning, communication, and emotions, and with the origins and fate of human relationships, while Bion pursued these themes in his psychoanalytic writings. Beckett and Bion had come up with certain problems that Bion called the protomental – an area in which physical and psychological functions cannot be separated. There was a parallel attempt to illuminate the kernel of this dark and terrifying psychic realm. Bion, based on the notion of 'not-been-born' and alongside it, developed the concept of the 'imaginary twin' (Bion, 1974). The imaginary twin is about a patient who in fantasy had prevented an imaginary twin from being born and who, as a consequence, was punished by this unborn psychic double by not being completely born himself. This patient said he felt as if he were 'in the womb', and Bion suggested that 'he feared being born'. Many patients present for therapy feeling depressed and with a sense of futility. On exploration the therapist often discovers a hidden but extremely powerful belief that one should not have been born, and a sense that one does not have the right to exist. The imaginary twin complex as identified by Bion and other dimensions of it are also frequent problems the therapist encounters in his practice. For instance, there are patients who have a very close bond with a sibling. One such patient has often complained about a sense of rejection whenever his senior sibling (one year older) has been paid more attention to than himself, whether by parents, other siblings, friends or lovers. For some time we have worked through the Oedipal connotations, the Bermuda Triangle in which the patient always seems to feel swallowed up, rejected and abandoned, while consumed with pain, hurt, envy, jealousy, murderous feelings and rivalry. However, the work has led us to the realization that there was something even more unconscious going on. I put it to him that the real pain at those times was to do with the realization that his sibling "is not his twin", for he is actually Other. It is this separation, otherness, not me, not my twin, not mine, that creates excruciating pain. This situation is more primitive than a triangular relationship, in that it is a two-person symbiotic relationship.

If the notion of 'not-been-born' was Jung's original idea, the connection of the not-been-born theme with the example of the imaginary twin is Bion's original creation. The personification of the imaginary twin, according to Bion, represents a defence structure against an intolerable emotional intensity and expresses an attempt to bridge the gap to reality (Bion, 1974).

One could perhaps hypothesize that Bion and Beckett were the imaginary twins, in that the other represented his secret soul–twin, the 'complementary double' who constituted a decisive stage in the creative process (of both). One may wonder, however, if the notion of the imaginary twin was not already implicit in Freud's discussion of Anna O, and other hysteric patients who seemed to have two personalities, one of which they knew about, and the other of which they knew nothing about, but which manifested in dreams and altered states of mind. Similarly, Jung himself was sure that his own mother consisted of two personalities, one innocuous and human, the other uncanny. In her personality number 1 she was a good mother: warm, pleasant, with a good sense of humour, and a fine cook, and inclined to look up to her son as he grew older, confiding in him, instead of his father, but her personality number 2 was a different matter: a sombre, imposing figure possessed by unassailable authority. Jung's mother, Emilie, came from a long line of seers. Her own mother had two personalities: a good monk and a bad monk, and she had visions and saw ghosts. Jung believed that he himself might be two different people, that is, as a child he recognized that he had a personality which was split: sure and unsure, optimistic and pessimistic, introverted and extroverted, sensitive and insensitive, brilliant and obtuse; genial yet given to violent rages; cold under warm, dark under light – always split, and that split always hidden, secret. Later on he called them 'Personality Number 1' and 'Personality Number 2', but growing up he hardly knew the difference. Personality number 1 was to the fore and lived more in the present, active at school and out and about in Basel. Personality number 2 was never far away: the unsure boy and the 'Other' the sure and powerful one. Not only did this other Carl exist, he was an old man, wore buckled shoes and a white wig and drove about in a fly with high wheels and a box suspended on springs with leather straps: a man living in the eighteenth century. The one as real as the other. One wonders if human beings do not all walk alongside 'a twin', although perhaps with much less imagination than Jung.

In the house where Jung's family moved when he was five, there was an old wall in the garden made of large blocks of stone and in the gaps between the stones he lit small fires which had an 'unmistakable aura of sanctity' about them and had to burn 'for ever'. One stone jilted out of the wall – 'My stone', he called it. Often when he was alone, he sat down on this stone, and then began an imaginary game that went something like this: 'I am sitting on top of this stone and it is underneath', but the stone could also say 'I' and think: 'I am lying here on this slope and he is sitting on top of me'. The question then arose: 'Am I the one who is sitting on the stone, or Am I the stone on which he is sitting?' This question always perplexed Jung, and he would stand up, wondering who was what now. The answer remained totally unclear, and his uncertainty was accompanied by a feeling of curious and fascinating darkness. However, there was no doubt whatsoever that this stone stood in some secret relationship to him. He could sit on it for hours, fascinated by the puzzle it set him. He sat on that stone for hours, trying to work out whether it was him, or he was it.

Many patients entertain the fantasy of self-contradictory objects. For instance, they can regard the analyst (and others) who is actually present as also the place were the analyst is not. Conversely, the analyst who is actually absent is regarded as a space which is occupied by the absent analyst (transformation in hallucinosis, in Bion's terms). Absence can be a negative presence and presence a negative absence. The object exists and does not exist. Plato's missing fourth in the *Timaeus* is not there and yet, he is fully present. The patient may identify himself with such an object and the contradiction then lies in his existing sufficiently to feel that he does not exist. Plato's (1997) *Parmenides* captured this intuition long ago: "A thing can never be unless it is both, is, and is not". For Plato non-being is a form of being. Some patients achieve a state of 'non-existence' briefly and then it is followed by an externalization or evacuation of 'non-existence'. 'Non-existence' immediately becomes an object that is hostile and filled with murderous envy towards the quality or function of existence wherever it is to be found. Others seem to exist in a perpetual state of non-existence, of not having been born. This notion is also closely linked to Winnicott's 'discontinuity of going on being', to Bion's 'nameless dread', and to Green's 'Dead Mother Complex' (1983). They all seem to refer to the feeling of non-existence, not having been born, to having been 'aborted', or on the brink of annihilation, and to not having a right to exist. These feelings are often intertwined with feelings of self-righteousness and a sense of entitlement.

Mr. D often complains of not having been born – emotionally, psychologically – and of not having been asked to be born. When he tells me that "he only feels he has a right to exit with me", I feel moved and narcissistically gratified, but also imprisoned and annihilated. It feels as if I do not have a right to have a separate existence from him, or my own identity. In pondering about this experience, I realize how frequently I have encountered this state of affairs with patients over the years. A sense of 'not having been born' might be much more pervasive than the extreme pathological implications of this state of mind seemed to imply. The fact is that this is a state of existence that applies to some people some of the time, and to others all of the time. In this context it is ironical that the *Timaeus* starts in absence and then Plato goes on to describe the creation or birth of the universe. It might well be that the most fundamental role of the psychotherapist is to provide a container for unborn aspects of the patient, or for the whole personality to be born. This is the emergent container of the analytic couple in relationship and dialogue.

References

Beckett, S. (1976). *For to End Yet Again and Other Fizzles.* London: John Cabler.
Bion, W. R. (1963). Elements of psycho-analysis. *Seven Servants.* New York: Jason Aronson, 1977.
Bion, W. R. (1965). Transformations. *Seven Servants.* New York: Jason Aronson, 1977.
Bion, W. R. (1974). *Bion's Brazilian Lectures,* 2. London: Karnac, 1990.
Bion, W. R. (1975–1978). *Four Discussions with W. R. Bion.* London: Clunie Press.
Deleuze, G., and Guattari, F. (1987). *A Thousand Plateaus: Capitalism and Schizophrenia.* Translated by B. Massumi. Minneapolis: University of Minnesota Press.
Donne, J. (1624). *Devotions upon Emergent Occasions. Meditation* XVII. Oxford: Oxford University Press, 1975.
Freud, S. (1900). The interpretation of dreams. *Standard Edition, 4, 5.*
Green, A. (1983). *The Dead Mother.* Edited by K. Mollon. London: Taylor & Francis e-Library, 2005.
Jung, C. G. (1935). The Tavistock Lectures. Collected Works, vol. *18.*
Kant, I. (1781). *First Critique of Pure Reason.* Translated by W. S. Phuhar. Indianapolis: Hackett (1966).
Lambert, K. (1981). *Analysis, Repair and Individuation.* London: Academic Press.
Plato. (1965). *Timaeus and Critias.* Translated by D. Lee. London: Penguin.
Whitehead, A. N. (1929). *Process and Reality.* Corrected ed., D. R. Griffin and D. W. Sherburne, Eds. New York: The Free Press, 1985.
Whitehead, A. N. (1933). *Adventure of Ideas.* New York: The Free Press, 1967.
Whitehead, A. N. (1938). *Modes of Thought.* New York: The Free Press, 1968.
Winnicott, D. W. (1949). Mind and its relation to soma. *British Journal of Medical Psychology, 27, 201–209.*
Winnicott, D. W. (1971). *Playing and Reality.* London: Pelican Books, 1974.

Index

Tavistock Lectures (Jung) 21–23, 46–47,
   65, 165, 185
Theaetetus (Plato) 82, 83
theory of knowing, Bion's 62–65
theory of prehension 81
theory of thinking, Bion's: absence and
   46–62; alpha-function theory 53;
   beta-elements (first thoughts) 46,
   51, 53, 59; bizarre objects 51;
   container-contained concept 47,
   48–49, 55; evacuative origin of
   thought 52; hallucinations 56–58;
   hallucinosis 58–61; Oedipus myth
   47–48; paranoid-schizoid/depressive
   positions, interaction between 55;
   pre-conceptions 47, 54; projective
   identification 46, 47, 48–51;
   psychological birth of the Self 50;
   psychotic/non-psychotic personality
   parts 51–52; theory of knowing 62–65;
   thought as prior to thinking 53–54
therapists: as containers 184–185; desire
   49–50, 87–88, 90; failure by 94–95,
   108; memory 49–50, 87–88, 90; as
   receptacle 11
thinking, Bion's theory of: absence and
   46–62; alpha-function theory 53;
   beta-elements (first thoughts) 46,
   51, 53, 59; bizarre objects 51;
   container-contained concept 47,
   48–49, 55; evauative origin of thought
   52; hallucinations 56–58; hallucinosis
   58–61; Oedipus myth 47–48;
   paranoid-schizoid/depressive
   positions, interaction between 55;
   pre-conceptions 47, 54; projective
   identification 46, 47, 48–51;
   psychological birth of the Self 50;
   psychotic/non-psychotic personality
   parts 51–52; thought as prior to
   thinking 53–54
thinking, Heidegger on 142–143
'third object' 73
thought feelings 72
Timaeus and Critias (Plato) 69, 77, 82,
   92, 139, 161, 163, 184, 188, 189;
   Atlantis as conceptualization of Self
   36–37; as myth-making of creation 12;

novelty in experience 35; opening 7, 9,
   70, 155; Plato's receptacle 7, 14, 163;
   quaternio 155; receptacle 9–10, 183
togetherness in experience 105
transcendent function 84, 85
transference, importance of 10–11,
   175–176
transformational object 166–168
transformations, Bion on 145–152
transitional object 73–78, 95, 96, 153
transitional space 14

uncertainty, tolerance of 55–56
unconscious infection 10

"Vala: Night the Second" (Blake) 93

waking and dreaming, balanced attitude
   between 94
Whitehead, A. N. 11, 26, 32, 64, 157, 159,
   169, 183–184; as act of imagination 57;
   causal efficacy 112–117, 141–142,
   172–173; concrescence 107, 114, 125,
   159, 177; and Deleuze on interrelations
   176–177; freshness in experience 35;
   imaging, hallucination as 35; impact of
   absence on 36–37; interconnections
   and independence 177–179; on
   interrelations 172–176; laughter 39;
   misplaced concreteness 20–21, 143; on
   nature 156; negative capability 92, 93;
   ontology 112–117; organism,
   philosophy of 113; Plato's oncology and
   117–119; on Plato's receptacle 12–15,
   183; prehensions 102, 104, 111, 112,
   172–173; receptivity 86; theory of
   prehension 81; *see also* experience;
   Heraclitus, Whitehead and
Winnicott, D. W. 11, 14, 33, 47, 58, 69,
   108, 133, 135, 137, 143, 144, 148,
   179–180, 183, 188; creativity 127–128;
   formless experience 169; transitional
   object 73–78, 95, 96, 153
woman, symbolic meaning of the
   vessel 23

Yeats, W. B. 94

For Product Safety Concerns and Information please contact our EU
representative GPSR@taylorandfrancis.com
Taylor & Francis Verlag GmbH, Kaufingerstraße 24, 80331 München, Germany

www.ingramcontent.com/pod-product-compliance
Lightning Source LLC
Chambersburg PA
CBHW050651280326
41932CB00015B/2867